The Heritage of India Series

Bengali Religious Lyrics, Sakta

The Heritage of India Series

Bengali Religious Lyrics, Sakta

Selected and Translated

BY

EDWARD J. THOMPSON,

LECTURER IN BENGALI, UNIVERSITY OF OXFORD;
AUTHOR OF "RABINDRANATH TAGORE, HIS LIFE AND WORK," ETC.

AND'

ARTHUR MARSHMAN SPENCER

GYAN

Published by

GYAN

Gyan Publishing House
5, Ansari Road
Daryaganj, New Delhi-110002
Phone: 011-47034999, 9811692060
E-mail: books@gyanbooks.com

Distribution Network
gyanbooks.com
India, USA, Canada, UK, Australia, France

ISBN : 978-81-212-2094-1 (PB)
First Published, 1923

2nd Impression 2021

Printed at: Gyan Press, Delhi.

The Heritage of India Series
Bengali Religious Lyrics Sakta
Selected and Translated by: Edward J. Thompson & Arthur Marshman Spencer

THE HERITAGE OF INDIA SERIES

Bengali Religious Lyrics, Sākta

Selected and Translated

BY

EDWARD J. THOMPSON,

LECTURER IN BENGALI, UNIVERSITY OF OXFORD;
AUTHOR OF "RABINDRANATH TAGORE, HIS LIFE AND WORK," ETC.,

AND

ARTHUR MARSHMAN SPENCER

ASSOCIATION PRESS
(Y.M.C.A.)
5, RUSSELL STREET, CALCUTTA

LONDON: OXFORD UNIVERSITY PRESS
NEW YORK, TORONTO, MELBOURNE,
BOMBAY, CALCUTTA AND MADRAS

1923

TRANSLATORS' PREFACE

THESE versions were first made from bazar-texts, the corrupt, irresponsible texts that swarm from Indian presses. We have had access to a better text lately, the best available, but it is not a good one. A scholarly edition of Rāmprasād is badly wanted.

We have received generous help. Dr. Brajendranath Seal discussed with us many of these songs, both in letters and conversation. Dr. Dineshchandra Sen has given valuable information. Professors Pramodekumar Banerji and Ramsaran Ghosh, our colleagues at the Wesleyan College, Bankura, and Babu Sasibhusan Ghosh, have gone over the original and notes with us. Babu Jnanendranath Sen has given permission to use four *Āgāmanī* songs by his father, the late Rajanikānta Sen.

Rāmprasād's songs are the great bulk of this selection. His eminence makes this right, especially as his songs are constantly imitated by other poets. But, if the Śākta literature of Bengal is to be appreciated, a fuller selection is needed than we have space for. Bengali scholars must first collect and edit this scattered literature; till this is done, our selection may serve a purpose.

Orthography proves a more difficult question every year. Such words as Brāhman and *svadeśī* may be taken as now anglicised into Brahmin and *swadeshi*. The Sanskrit orthography misrepresents Bengali, but is a convenience to scholars. We have given it on the first occurrence of a Bengali word. But we have non-conformed in the spelling of some Bengali places and of Rāmprasād. If the poet is Rāmprasād to the fifty millions of his compatriots, and if Ravindranātha Ṭhakura is allowed to call himself Rabindranath, not only in Bengali but in English, we think Rāmprasād Sen should be saved from becoming Rāmaprasāda Sena. Titles of poems are our own.

CONTENTS

INTRODUCTION

THE ritual of all the greater gods and goddesses of modern Hinduism is the result of a syncretism extending over at least three milleniums. The figures of the gods of Vedic times have receded, till to-day Indra, once the greatest, has only one temple in all India; Varuṇa has dwindled into being lord of the sea, an element which touches the life of India hardly at all; and Agni has become a kind of nobler *lar domesticus*. Their place has been filled by deities whose principal names, in some cases, are not even mentioned in the Vedas. Vishṇu, in his *avatārs* as Rāma and Kṛishṇa, and Śiva divide the allegiance of the vast majority of Hindus. This allegiance is further divided, by the existence of *Śāktas*, worshippers of the female energy, *śakti*, of these deities. Their worship is an expression of the age-long Hindu recognition of a dual principle in nature, *purusha* (male) and *prakṛiti* (female). For practical purposes, *Śāktism* may be regarded as the worship of Durgā or Kālī, Śiva's consort. About this worship a vast jungle of ritual has grown up, and scholars will probably always be occupied with the effort to disentangle this or that brake of ritual, and to identify its original root. Pārvatī, daughter of Himālaya; Umā, the gracious and (as Satī) self-immolating wife; Kālī the terrible; Durgā 'the unapproachable,' less terrible than Kālī—these are all manifestations of the one goddess, Śiva's consort. Kālī and Durgā may be originally goddesses of the savage tribes whom the Aryans found lurking in inaccessible forests; Pārvatī may be a mountain deity—these matters may be studied elsewhere. Their names do not occur in the Vedas.

Śiva—called by many names, Mahādeva, 'The Great God'; Bhairava, 'The Terrible One'—is the Destroyer.

He is the great Ascetic, with matted locks, seated in age-long meditation, or haunting burning-grounds, wandering fiercely, accompanied by ghosts and goblins. At first sight, it might seem that no more repellent deity could be imagined; but there is so much of sublimity in the conception of him that many of the most religious Hindus have been attracted by his figure. It is easy to understand and to share this attraction. The dreadful need not be immoral, and it can be, often is, sternly bracing, as well as wildly poetical. All men in the end must come to the burning-ground; and the God who is a destructive fire, shrivelling to ashes all that is transitory and fleshly, who is divine negligence personified, meditating amid the ruin of worlds or wandering among the cinders which are all that is left of men's hopes and passionate love—all except memory, growing ever fainter as the years pass—this God in the mind's bleaker moods may bring such sad exultation and courage as men have felt on a lost battlefield or amid eternal snows.

But much of Śiva's worship has gone to his consort, Kālī or Durgā. Possibly because it was felt necessary to remove the God beyond the operation of *karma* or activity, logically involving change and consequences, within the first millenium of the Christian era the tendency grew up to centralise and intensify his energies in his śakti or female counterpart. Vishṇu, too, has his śakti, as have all the gods; but it is round the names of Kālī and Durgā that the great bulk of Śākta worship has gathered. The manuals of this worship are the Tantras, whose number is variously estimated. Hundreds have been lost, but very many survive.[1] Parts of the Purāṇas also deal with the Śākta cult. The whole cult is very obscure, partly because it enjoins the strictest secrecy; but it is known that in its worst forms it is perhaps the vilest and most degraded worship that has ever been. Śiva is not only destroyer, but lord of

[1] See Farquhar, *Outline of the Religious Literature of India*, *passim*. For much of this and the next paragraph, I have taken this book as my authority.

reproduction, and his worship is most widespread in its phallic form, the adoration of the *liṅga*. But that symbol has been so changed from its true shape that the sight of it does not do the evil that might be expected. It is otherwise with the worst side of śakti-worship.

Durgā is first mentioned in the *Mahābhārata*,[1] in a passage where she is the sister of Kṛishṇa, like him dark-blue in colour; she upholds heaven by her chastity, lives in the Vindhya mountains, and delights in wine, flesh, and animal sacrifice. Presently we find her 'definitely made the wife of Śiva,"[2] and addressed as Umā, the gentle and propitious. In later legend, she destroys demons and giants, devours the flesh of her enemies and drinks blood. The Durgā-pūjā is the great festival of Bengal, when friends and families come together. Durgā's image is decorated; on the sixth day she is awakened; on the night of the eighth day countless goats and some buffaloes are sacrificed to her. Many families, however, especially Vaishṇava ones, celebrate the pūjā with bloodless sacrifices of sugarcane or pumpkins, severed in half in one blow, just as the living victims are decapitated with one stroke. One great family offers a single betel-nut, which is laid before the image, and then sacrificed by a blacksmith who has been practising the feat of exact division in two for the past three months, and receives a hundred rupees for his services. In other cases, all pretence of 'sacrifice' is dropped and flowers are offered. The pūjā seems to be growing yearly gentler in spirit. The goddess keeps her ten arms and weapons of menace, but the latter are hidden with tinsel and lotuses; the face is benign, and the whole figure is made beautiful. Fewer goats are sacrificed, fewer houses have their own images, the pūjā becoming less of a worship, and much more just a national holiday of great happiness.

To Durgā as Kālī, human sacrifices used to be offered, before their prohibition by the British Government.

[1] IV, vii.
[2] Farquhar, *op. cit.*, 150.

The Thugs, robbers who mixed with travellers and then strangled them in lonely places, regarded their victims as sacrificed to Kālī.

In the Śākta-cult, the worst side of Kālī-worship culminates. Of its two sects, the 'right-hand Śāktas' do not practise the more evil ritual. The worship of the 'left-hand Śāktas' is done in secret, usually at night. It consists of partaking of the *five tattvas, i.e. realities,*[1] *viz.* wine, meat, fish, parched grain, and sexual intercourse. Sometimes a naked woman represents the goddess. The worshippers are an equal number of men and women, of any caste, and may be near relations. These rites, and the human character built upon them, have been pictured for us by Bankimchandra Chatterji, in a book which is one of the master-examples of the shorter novel, *Kapālakuṇḍalā*. The picture is drawn, without revolt or sympathy, in the detached spirit of Art, by one who was in most things a conservative Hindu.

The left-hand Śākta-cult, in addition to its sacrificial and sexual features, is distinguished by a very extensive practice of magic. This is partly built upon a fantastic physiology. The human frame contains an immense number of channels of occult force, the chief of them being the *sushumṇā* in the spinal cord. The occult force is centralised in six circles. In the lowest of these, the goddess lies asleep, coiled three and a half times round a liṅga, serpent-fashion. She can be awakened by Śākta-yoga or Śākta-meditation, and induced to ascend to the highest circle. When asleep in the lowest circle, the *mūlādhāra*, the goddess is called Kuṇḍalinī, 'The coiled one.'[2] These circles and channels of occult force are sources of miraculous power to the initiated. The Tantras contain many detailed instructions in sorcery, which was practised in early times. In the *Mālatī-Mādhava*, a drama composed in the eighth century by Bhavabhūti, the famous Sanskrit poet, we are taken 'in the twilight to the burning-ground, fetid with the fumes

[1] *Tattva* means the underlying truth or substance.
[2] See No. XXX of this Book.

of the funeral pyre.'[1] There the hero Mādhava comes, 'his hair ceremonially braided, a sword in one hand and a piece of human flesh in the other. He has come to invoke the disembodied spirits that haunt the spot, hoping to barter the human flesh for supernatural power to aid him in winning Mālatī.'[1]

Śākta hymns contain many references to both the philosophy and the practice of the cult. Such references will be found in the hymns of Rāmprasād in this book, though we have tried always to give the most intelligible translation of a passage, and not to trouble the reader with a subtle and sometimes dull, occasionally disgusting, significance. But the better side of Śāktism is the one which is generally present in Rāmprasād. Further, it should be very clearly borne in mind that, even among the left-hand Śāktas, probably very few practise the extreme cult. The great majority of Hindus regard that extreme cult with abhorrence. Many Bengalis would not understand every allusion, even in Rāmprasād.

The worship of Durgā and Kālī is perhaps most deeply rooted in Bengal, as has already been indicated. I think it would not be hard to find reasons for this. Take the case of a celebrated predecessor of Rāmprasād, Mukundarāma, known as Kavikaṅkaṇ or 'gem of poets,' who finished his chief poem, the epic *Chaṇḍī*, in 1589. This poem lives today mainly for its value as giving a picture of the village-life of Bengal, three centuries ago. It is at present being edited by a distinguished Bengali scholar and author, who tells me he finds his work very dull; happier times have robbed the poem of much of its appeal. For the poet lived in an unhappy age. In some respects, he is like a Bengali Langland, giving us his vision of Piers Plowman. The local Musalman rulers practised great oppression, and the people felt wretched and helpless. It was natural for them to look for outside assistance, and the thoughts of the poet, their spokesman, turned to Chaṇḍī (Durgā), the powerful goddess in whom the dreadful energy of

[1] *Outline of the Religious Literature of India*, pp. 203-4.

Śiva was active. In *Chaṇḍī* the beasts of the forest complain to the goddess that they are in terror of Kālaketu the hunter. Under the guise of their speeches and of Chaṇḍī's, the political state of Bengal is set out.

Today, men are feeling too proud to consent to be wretched or to despair. Rabindranath Tagore, as is well known, is no lover of Śāktism; and, like many patriotic Bengalis, he feels that the time for such an attitude as Mukundarāma's has passed. 'The poet was a poor man, and was oppressed. So his only refuge was in the thought of this capricious Power, who might suddenly fling down the highest and exalt the lowest.'[1] It is interesting in this connection to notice that the great period of Śākta-poetry in Bengal was the end of the eighteenth century, when the country's fortunes had reached their lowest ebb, and were about to turn towards prosperity. It is true that Śākta-poetry is written today; but if we would see the adoration of the terrible goddess in all its sincerity and passion, we must go back to the eighteenth century, to the period when the Bengali mind became so unhappy and so darkened, when men died and despaired so easily, and when the number of satīs[2] increased to such a grim extent, in the last half-century before the rite was abolished. The cult of Kālī received another great revival in the days of the *swadeshi* struggle, within the present century, when the thought of the educated classes began to be consolidated in the demand for the control of their own destinies. There was a strong attempt to identify it with nation-worship; Kālī was held to be Bengal personified. This aspect of the cult is perhaps not very far below the surface even now. But there has come such an access of mental happiness and of self-respect to the people, that it is certain that they will not again feel as despondent as the poet of *Chaṇḍī* did, with no hope but from the intervention and irruption of sudden, irresponsible power. At least, it will be unreasonable if they do.

[1] Conversation. [2] Suttees.

This view of the reason (in part) for the prevalence of Kālī-worship is, I think, borne out elsewhere than in Bengal. Kālī was the tutelary goddess of Chitor. She has her blood-blackened shrines still on the deserted plateau where only the crumbling temples and palaces remain. No legend of Chitor is better-known or more impressive than that which tells how a giant form was seen between the pillars of the *rāṇā's* house. 'I am hungry,' said the goddess; and demanded that twelve who bore the crown of Chitor must perish. And (we are told) eleven of the king's twelve sons and the king himself assumed brief rule and perished in battle. The world has never seen more devoted soldiers than the Rajputs of Chitor. But their history shows that they despaired very quickly. A walk round their astounding defences, in one spectator at least—who had seen a good many battles—raised admiration for the skill and courage that could take such a fortress, against such defenders. Nothing but the conviction, that some Power was crying for their blood, and that they were doomed, could have brought them to such a resolved helplessness as made them three times send their women to the funeral-pyre and themselves to death outside the walls.

But it is not political distress alone that makes men's minds gloomy. After many years' residence in the poorest district in Bengal, I have felt there is some sorrow deeper and more permanent; the peasant is fighting a losing battle. One year the heavens are shut and there is drought. The rivers are empty sands. Famine follows; and incalculable misery. The next year it rains in excess, and the vast watercourses swell with huge floods. The streams feel their way along their banks till they come to the sandhead which blocks an old course—Bengal is full of these 'blind rivers,' as they are called. Here the water checks a moment, like a darkened mind groping and feeling. Some dim memory stirs that once, it may be a century ago, the way was here; then the waters gather together, and plunge through. A village two miles from the main river, living in security all these years, beside its 'blind river,' will wake at midnight to find a shoreless sea heaving and thrusting at the mud walls. This experience may be repeated, not once, but often in one Rains, as if Nature were an ogress, watching till the folk had put together some makeshift shelter of palm-leaves and mud, to dash it to ground again. So the long, bitter fight goes on. The people, after centuries of this, have become patient, uncomplaining, hopeless. I am speaking of the villages. It was in the villages that Rāmprasād and the poet of *Chaṇḍī* lived: Calcutta is a different world. But there come years when Nature seems caressing, indeed a Mother; when the rain is neither too much nor too little, but just sufficient. The fields are filled, the mud huts stand. It is not strange that Bengal should think of God as a Mother; yet, as Rāmprasād's songs show, should think of her with fear, as capricious and sometimes terribly cruel. It is to this Mother that the Śākta-poets have turned; for, as Rāmprasād reminds us frequently, her lord is Bhōlānātha, 'lord of forgetfulness,' the God who wanders abstractedly or sinks into meditation. There is little chance of help in him. Śakti has all his dreadful power, and her energy is unsleeping.

Not much is known of Rāmprasād. He was born at Kumārhātī, near Hālisahar, in 1718. His birthplace is within the old bounds of Nadiyā, a district which is the very heart and metropolis of Bengal's life and history. From here it was that Lakshmaṇ Sen, its last independent king, fled before the Musalmans; it was in this district that the great court of the Rajas of Kṛishṇagar, centuries later, kept art and poetry alive. Śileidā, the favourite retreat of Bengal's most famous poet today, is in Nadiyā.

Rāmprasād was the son of Rāmrām Sen. His descendants today are Vaidyas by caste, and in his poems he refers to himself as a Vaidya;[1] but it has sometimes been asserted that he was a Brahmin. He

[1] The physician caste.

received some education; knew some Sanskrit, Persian, and Hindī, and, when a very young man, obtained a post in Calcutta, as copyist with Vakulachandra Ghōsāl, the *dewān* (manager) of an estate. Like other poets before and since, he found officework irksome, and he filled his books with scribbled verses. His employer discovered this, and was angry; but when he read, 'I do not want this copyist's work. Give me your treasuryship, Mother,' his sense of humour or his sense of piety overcame his annoyance. He became a generous friend and patron, settling on the poet a pension of Rs. 30 (£3, according to the reckoning of John Company days) a month, and introducing him to the Kṛishṇagar Court. Here Rāmprasād rose in favour, and won the title of Kavirañjana or 'Entertainer of Poets.' He had a rival, one Aju Goswāmī, a Vaishṇava. We do not know much about their relations with one another, but they seem to have been kindly. Rāmprasād wrote, on one occasion, 'Free me from the net of *Māyā* (Illusion), Mother'; to which his far from ascetic compeer replied with the prayer, 'Bind me in its wide chains.'

His fame was well established in his lifetime, and there are many legends about him. To one of these he laughingly refers in No. LVI of this selection. Others are obviously of later date, invented to explain the genesis of this or that poem. For instance: on his way to the Ganges, he met a woman who asked him to sing to her. He told her to wait at his house, till he returned from bathing. When he arrived and asked for her, she had gone, but had left a note for him in the family temple. This note informed him that the goddess Kālī had come from Kāśī (Benares) to hear him sing, and now commanded him to go to Kāśī. He fell ill on the road, and composed the song, 'I cannot go, but your Feet shall be my Kāśī.' Recovering, he tried to go on; but fell ill again, and saw Kālī in vision, telling him to forgo the journey. He obeyed her, making the song which is No. XV in this book.

Rāmprasād had friends and patrons in Calcutta, and often visited the town. He died in 1775. The older tradition was that the night of his death he worshipped Kālī and composed the song, 'Tārā, do you remember any more.'[1] Then he died singing, like Saxon Caedmon; with the conclusion of the lyric, his soul 'went out through the top of his head,' and passed to the World of Brahman, whence there is no return to this wearisome cycle of births and deaths. But Dr. Dineshchandra Sen, the historian of Bengali Language and Literature, tells me he has ascertained that Rāmprasād, following in a trance the clay image of Kālī, when it was thrown into the Ganges, on the Kālīpūjā day, was drowned. He adds, 'The old men of our country, altogether devoid of any historical sense, created fables out of anything they could lay their hands on, in the poems themselves, for lack of reliable information. The Sanskrit poetic canons have laid it down that unfortunate events in the life of a great man should not be narrated. Thus, the true accounts of the death of Chaṇḍīdās, who was killed by the order of an Emperor of Gaur, of Chaitanya, who died of an inflammatory fever caused by a sore, of Godādhar, who was burnt alive by the Muhammadans, have not been recorded by our biographers, and the truth has been hidden by wild legendary fables.'

Rāmprasād's works, other than his *Śākta* songs, are the *Bidyāsundar* (*Vidyāsundara*) *Kālīkīrtan*,[2] *Śivasaṅkīrtan* and *Kṛishṇakīrtan*: the last three are very short, a few pages. The theme of the *Bidyāsundar* is an old Bengali story. The Rājā of Burdwan had a daughter[3] famous for her learning and her beauty. He vowed she should not wed anyone but her superior in learning. The Rājā of Kāñchī's son obtained access to her, married her by the so-called 'Gāndharva'[4] rites—

[1] See No. LXV.

[2] *Kīrtan* means a processional song or hymn. Two pieces from the *Kālīkīrtan* (LXXXIX and XC) are given in this book.

[3] Her name was *Vidyā* (learning) and her lover's *Sundara* (beautiful).

[4] The marriage which took place between Dushyanta and Śakuntalā, in Kālidāsa's play, and between Arjuna and Chītrāṇgadā, in Tagore's.

which were just physical union, neither more nor less—and then publicly vanquished her (by her connivance) in learning. Rāmprasād's well-known contemporary, Bhāratchandra Ray, the *rājkavi* or *king's poet* of Kṛishṇagar, wrote a better poem with the same theme and title, his treatment being erotic and grossly indecent. Rāmprasād allegorises the story; even so, the poem is not one of which his admirers are proud.

But the Śākta poems are a different matter. These have gone to the heart of a people as few poets' work has done. Such songs as the exquisite 'This day will surely pass, Mother, this day will pass,' I have heard from coolies on the road or workers in the paddy fields; I have heard it by broad rivers at sunset, when the parrots were flying to roost and the village folk thronging from marketing to the ferry. Once I asked the top class in a mofussil[1] high school to write out a song of Rabindranath Tagore's; two boys out of forty succeeded, a result which I consider showed the very real diffusion of his songs. But, when I asked for a song of Rāmprasād's, every boy except two responded. Truly, a poet who is known both by work and name to boys between fourteen and eighteen, is a national poet. Tagore's songs are heard in Calcutta streets, and have been widely spread by the student community and the Brahmo Samaj; but in the villages of Bengal they are unknown, while Rāmprasād's are heard everywhere. 'The peasants and the *paṇḍits* enjoy his songs equally. They draw solace from them in the hour of despair and even at the moment of death. The dying man brought to the banks of the Ganges asks his companions to sing Rāmprasādī songs.'[2]

Sister Nivedita compared Rāmprasād with Blake. He resembles rather Herrick, in his self-consciousness and his habit of looking at himself from outside. But these are only casual and partial affinities. His lyrics at their simplest often have the quality of a snatch of

[1] Roughly rural as opposed to urban or metropolitan. Anglicized in India, and spelt accordingly by me.

[2] Dr. Sen, in a letter to me.

nursery babble, and sing themselves into the memory of an illiterate folk by a riot of punning sound and alliteration, a musical toss and play of similar syllables.[1] Rāmprasād took a childlike pleasure in these, and that untrained literary instinct out of which folklore and folksong are born, takes the same pleasure and has heard him with rapture. Much of his imagery is fanciful and conceited, and of anything but universal validity; yet even this has a charm, examined with patience and sympathy. The student of his poetry will be rewarded with a wealth of local thought and custom and of such stories as flower in the undergrowth and by-ways of authorised legend. This 'local habitation' of Rāmprasād's mind is strength as well as sometimes weakness. His range of ideas and illustrations is narrow; but within that range he is a master. If he falls short on occasion, because so much of Tantric teaching is puerile and worthless, he rises greatly again when he touches Earth, that Universal Mother. His illustration is racy, from the soil and of the soil; it comes from the life of an agricultural people. In Bengal, 'every schoolboy' (as a matter of plain, literal fact) knows his sublimely simple reproof to his soul, in a moment's shrinking from death, 'Thou, a snake, fearing frogs.'[2] This wealth of metaphor plucked from a simple life and society will meet the reader on every page. His mind has been a bad farmer;[3] he is treading the Round of Existence, like the blindfold ox that serves the oilman,[4] chained to 'the log' of the world; the Six Passions, like crocodiles[5] haunting the bathing *ghāt*, watch for his soul; or they are robbers, leaping over the mud wall of his courtyard;[6] or they are hired bullies with clubs,[7] like the ruffians kept by Bengali rājās and squires; they are cowardly boatmen, who forsake the soul when the tempest sweeps up life's river.[8] Once upon a time he had house and friends, he earned money and he was popular, but now he is a

[1] This, of course, cannot be kept in translation.
[2] No. XLII. [3] No. XXVIII. [4] No. XXIX. [5] No. XXX.
[6] No. XXXII. [7] No. XXI. [8] No. XXXIV.

beggar and forsaken.[1] Very often his thought turns to life's finish, when his friends will leave him, bones and ashes on the burning-ground.

It is profitable to study the attitude of the remarkable poets of the people, which every century has produced, in every part of India. Indian philosophy has reasoned out certain conclusions; its typical expression, as everyone knows, is the Vedānta; and no one would deny that even the thought of the illiterate has a pantheistic tinge. This has often been pointed out. Perhaps too much has been made of it; men forget how St. Paul confidently looked to find at least this tinge, alike in the thought of idlers in the market-place at Athens and in that of Lystra peasants. If we study the folk-poets, and through them the mental outlook of the simple folk of India, we find vulgar thought often in absolute revolt from those findings of the philosophers so readily and dogmatically put forth in Europe as Indian belief. These are only one side of Indian belief. Tennyson has not expressed more incisively than Rāmprasād the rejection, by the mind that has loved, of the doctrine of loss of personal life. What is the use of salvation to me, cries Rāmprasād, if it means absorption? 'I like eating sugar, but I have no desire to become sugar.'[2] No thought anywhere—aware as he was of Śaṅkarāchārya's monism and in sympathy as some of his moods show him to be with pantheistic teaching—is more emphatically theistic than his normally is, or rests more decidedly upon interchange and intercourse between a personal goddess and a personal suppliant and worshipper. With the popular religious idolatry, and especially its crudities and cruelties, he has no part. He scoffs at pilgrimage, and offerings to images. 'I laugh when I hear that a worshipper of Kālī has gone to Gayā.'[3] He is sturdily ethical, will have nothing to do with the suggestion that good and evil are the same thing, philosophically considered. He is terrified of those six passions who leap

[1] No. XX. [2] No. XV. [3] *Ibid.*

over his life's low wall. In a passage famous with his countrymen, he looks past the bloodstained image which represents his 'Mother' to the many, sees with revolt the butchered victims and the red stains upon the flowers of worship, and cries out to that World-Mercy which he has found for himself and which he adores, that he will sacrifice not living, quivering flesh but the *Six Passions*, the sins of his heart and mind. This passage has never been forgotten by his countrymen; and, though some have disingenuously used it to buttress up the bloody system it condemns, representing their sacrifices as an acted allegory, the victims standing for the sins and passions, yet the naturally merciful thought of the most has seen his literal meaning, and has felt judged and unhappy, even though the slaughter may continue.

Living through that time of anarchy, when Bengal was at the mercy of thieves and oppressors of every race and sort, Rāmprasād kept his vision of Divine kindness, his trust in Divine love that was good despite all seeming. Kālī dancing on her lord, Kālī festooned with skulls, with lolling tongue black with blood, with dripping weapons uplifted and menacing eyes, is not a figure with which one would naturally associate such love as Rāmprasād's. Further, he was a Śākta, and practised the Śākta-yōga. But his poems leave the cruel, lustful side of Tantric worship on one side, their insistence on blood, especially human blood, and on intoxicating drink and the prostitution of maidenhood. His mind, when it touched upon the sterner aspects of the Śākta cult, leapt to those features that were sublime, though in lurid fashion. He saw Kālī in the red flames of the burning-ground, flickering and dancing in the breeze; in the flash of the lightning, or coming with the black, matted cloud-locks of the storm.[1] This terror, leading to imperfect trust, intrudes even into his love of Kālī as Mother. Though she beat it, he says, the child clings to its mother, crying *Mother*. Today the world's pain does not seem lightened if we

[1] See Sen, p. 715.

think of it as inflicted by a Hand external to it; our only hope is if we can see God identified with His children's sorrow. Of this conception there is no hint in Rāmprasād, and in this respect he falls short of the Musalman mystic who said, 'My Friend does me no wrong; the cup which he gives me to drink he has drunk before me,' or of the Tamil Māṇikka Vāsahar, who loved Śiva because

> 'Thou drankest poison black, the humbler beings pitying,
> That I, thy meanest one, might find no poison, but a nectar fount.'[1]

His mood is too monotonously one of complaint; it is that of a grey experience, with little hope or sunlight. Yet how much of purity and tenderness is in his songs! 'What folly is this in thee, the child of the Mother-Heart of All, fearing death! Thou, a snake, afraid of frogs!' Least of all should any Christian dare to marvel at the mercy which reached this man through such paths. For God, says St. John, is love. And love, says an old song, will find out the way.

The best edition of Rāmprasād, issued by the *Basumatī* office, Calcutta, contains 226 songs. This collection is far from complete; nor is the text authoritative. Tests of genuineness are various, mention of his name in the poem and the poem's setting to the 'Rāmprasādī' tune being chief. Some undoubtedly authentic songs exist both with and without his name; it is likely, then, that his name was sometimes added by other hands. Among our translations, we have included as his nearly a dozen songs that are not in the *Basumatī* collection; also, the fuller and more picturesque text of No. VII, which may possibly be a later writing-up. We have added another four songs—Nos. LXVI-LXIX—after those which we believe to be his; they are part of the extensive and hitherto unexamined Rāmprasād 'apocrypha.' They are often printed as his, and may be.

[1] *Hymns of Tamil Śaivite Saints*, Kingsbury and Phillips.

Later Śākta poetry imitates Rāmprasād a great deal. Kamalākānta Bhaṭṭāchārya came close to him in point of time, living in the last quarter of the eighteenth century and well into the nineteenth. Nothing much seems to be known of him; he removed from Ambikānagar, in the Khulnā district, to Kōtālhāṭā, in the Burdwan district, in 1800, and he was the religious preceptor of the Mahārājā of Burdwan. His Śākta poetry does not appear to deserve its reputation; out of his many songs we have given four. One of the best Śākta poets was Nīlakaṇṭha Mukhopādhyāya, a native of the village of Dharaṇī, in the Burdwan district, a district that has been a nurse of poets. Nīlakaṇṭha was a good singer, leader of a *jātrā* (*yātrā*)[1] which was very popular in West Bengal, thirty years ago. He was the author of numerous *Vaishṇava* and of over a hundred *Śākta* songs; these are sung throughout the Burdwan, Bānkurā and Birbhum districts. The reader will notice that No. LXXVIII is modern in tone, influenced by the teaching of Rāmkṛishṇa Paramhaṁsa, that all worshipped gods are the same. Nīlakaṇṭha died aged sixty; but no one apparently knows the dates of his birth or death, though many people now living met him, and his memory is cherished as that of a very simple-minded and attractive man. Of the poets represented in this book by one poem only, Mahārājā Rāmkṛishṇa, of Naṭōr, is the earliest; he was a contemporary of Rāmprasād. Rasikchandra Rāy (1820-1893), a voluminous writer of songs for *jātrās*, composed the well-known song which is No. LXXVI of this book. Rāmchandra Datta (1861-1899), author of No. LXXXI, was a doctor on the staff of the Medical College, Calcutta. In 1879, he began to visit Rāmkṛishṇa Paramhaṁsa, and joined his movement. By his extensive practice and his salary as a professor, he made a large income, most of which he spent in religious works.

The vast Śākta literature is monotonous with its four or five themes—Kālī's neglect of her votary, Śiva's

[1] Travelling theatrical party.

carelessness, the poet's threatened law-suits or desertion of the Mother, the Mother's absorption in her wild, destructive dance, her standing over 'the Lord of Death.' The Calcutta theatre has kept up, along with worse things, the vernacular tradition of piety, and Vaishṇava and Śākta songs find their way from the boards into remote villages, the gramophone being the effective agent in this dispersal. An excellent example of the modern spirit at work is provided by No. LXXXVIII. The author is a *baul*. *Bauls* are mendicant religious singers, often almost unlettered (though the author of No. LXXXVIII can hardly be that). The reader will note the echo of Rāmprasād's protest against sacrifices. But this comes with a new tenderness—the dumb victims are 'the Mother's children.' The poet's thought takes a larger sweep, for he belongs to the present, whose instincts and practice are both (whatever pessimists may allege) more compassionate than any former age has known. The song's atmosphere and teaching reflect the merciful and ethical theism which is to-day overspreading all lands. Its Bengali differentia is that it looks towards the motherhood, and not the fatherhood, of God.

This song fitly concludes our Śākta selection, carrying the thought of Rāmprasād into the world of today. It is followed by fifteen *Āgāmanī* and *Vijayā* songs, taken from different writers and arranged to form a drama of welcome and farewell. Two new writers of importance appear in this section. Dāśarathī Rāy, born at Bandāmura in the Burdwan district in 1804, died in 1857. He enjoyed immense popularity, most of his verses being improvised before delighted crowds. By his very clever and very indecent poetry, he made a considerable fortune. He was in the old vernacular tradition, untouched by English influence. No. XCIX, a beautiful song, shows him at his best. Rajanikānta Sen was born in 1865; he practised as a pleader at Rajshahi; and died in the Medical College, Calcutta, of cancer. His Āgāmanī poems were composed during his last illness, and published posthumously.

The theme and occasion of Āgāmanī and Vijayā songs are as follows. Umā or Gaurī, daughter of Himālaya and Menakā, was married to Śiva, the Lord of Kailāsa, at the age of eight. The fable has had this unfortunate consequence, that every attempt to raise the legal age for marriage has been opposed by conservative Hindus with the cry of 'Gaurī dān,' 'The giving of Gaurī,' and a peculiar blessing has been asserted to rest upon a girl's marriage at the age of eight. But it has also furnished an outlet for the loneliness and grief of parents mourning their daughters gone from them so early, who have found their own sorrow mirrored in the legendary sorrow of the Great Goddess's parents. Dr. Dinesh Sen says, speaking of of the marriage of very young girls to old men,[1] the situation created pathos too deep for expression. This situation, he suggests, is the real theme of the Āgāmanī poets. 'There are innumerable songs in Bengali, describing the pathetic situation. The domestic scenes of Bengal—the sorrows of Bengali parents—are really the themes of the songs, though they profess to deal with mythological subjects. . . . The girls here, of too tender an age to play the wife, are often taken away from the custody of parents. With veils over their faces, they have to stay in their husband's home, speak in whispers and subject themselves to the painful discipline of the daughter-in-law. . . . When the Āgāmanī songs, describing the sorrows of Menakā and of Umā, her daughter, are sung by professional singers, the eyes of many a child-wife glisten behind her veil, and the hearts of their mothers cry out for the daughters who have been taken away from them.'[2]

The Durgā-pūjā falls in late September or October. Some fifteen days before, Āgāmanī or 'advent' songs are heard everywhere. The pūjā begins on the sixth day of the moon, when Umā (Durgā) revisits her parents for three days. Those parents have discovered that their son-in-law, the Lord of Kailāsa, is a drug-

[1] *History of Bengali Language and Literature*, p. 841.
[2] *Ibid.*, p. 243. Dr. Sen's book is a mine of delightful reading.

eating vagabond, a haunter of waste places where dead men's bones lie; and their hearts go out in overflowing and distressed love to their child, returning to them, as once Persephone to Demeter from the gloomy throne of her dark consort. The whole pūjā is a very happy time, the Bengali Christmas. Small boys explode fireworks incessantly, to their own immense joy and the good-humoured annoyance of passers-by. There is feasting and reunion everywhere.

In these songs, the sorrows of Umā have passed away, from the region of religion, into that of poetry. Many of them are of great beauty; the reader will be struck by the way in which the goddess has been taken into the family and inner domesticities of the Bengali home. She has been adopted as a kind of divine daughter; and the incidents of her history with her strange Lord are told with a straightforward simplicity that is often delightful. This is carried even further in a number of songs (of which we give examples), which are not Āgāmanī songs, strictly speaking, but closely akin to them. Of these, a few deal with Umā's Lord, yet chiefly as being her Lord and not for his own sake. There is no such extensive Śiva-literature in Bengal as we find in South India; his consort, in her various manifestations, has largely absorbed his cult or attached it to her own. But there is at least one voluminous and very popular Śiva-poem, the *Śivāyana* by Rāmeśwara, written about 1750. In this, and in other poems of this class, Śiva's life in Kailāsa is shown. 'Umā in Kailāsa plays the house wife, the perfect prototype of the Hindu wife, ever accustomed to patient and strenuous self-denial and labour, cheerfully borne for the sake of others. Her highest delight lies in distributing food to her husband, children and servants.'[1] Dr. Sen translates (or, rather, paraphrases) a passage from the *Śivāyana*: 'With his two sons Śiva sits down to dine. Three sit to eat, and Umā serves food to them.[2] As soon as

[1] Sen, p. 246.

[2] Literally, 'Satī'—'The faithful wife,' here used as a name of Umā—'serves the food alone.'

she has served food, the plates are emptied, and they look into the cooking-pot. Padmāvatī[1] observes how eagerly Śiva eats, and smiles. Śukta[2] is finished, and they fall upon broth. Meantime the plates are all emptied of rice, and they all want more. "Mother!" says Kārttika, "Give us rice!" and Gaṇeśa also repeats the request, while the Lord of Destruction says, "O Umā, bring more rice." . . . Umā smiles, and distributes rice. Gaṇeśa says, "I have finished my curry, what more have you in store?" Hastily she comes, and serves ten different kinds of dried food. Śiva is much pleased, and praises her for her good cooking. The fried dhutarā[3] fruit and cups of siddhi[3] are given to the Great God, and he nods his head in approval as he sips. When all the curries are finished, they all call at the same time for more. . . . She finds it hard to serve so many. . . . She next serves pudding of pleasant flavour, and then a sauce both sweet and sour. Her hair becomes dishevelled, and her dress grows loose. With sweetmeats of milk and rice, the dinner ends."[4]

On the tenth day of the moon, the images of Durgā are thrown into the water, and people go from house to house, greeting their friends. This is the *Vijayā*[5] *milana*, or 'meeting together in victory,' festival. Vijayā songs, bidding farewell to Umā, who has already

[1] Umā's maid-servant.

[2] The first curry.

[3] The narcotics to which Śiva is addicted. *Dhutarā* (more correctly, dhutūrā) is datura; *Siddhi* is *cannabis sativa.*

[4] Sen, pp. 247-48.

[5] From *Vijayā*, *Victory*. But no one seems to know why the festival has this name. It is by some connected with Rāma's victory over Rāvana, after worshipping Durgā; by some with Durgā's own victory over the demon Mahishāsura. Neither explanation is convincing. Dr. Farquhar writes: 'In both the hymns to Durgā in the *Mahābhārata* she is called Jayā and Vijayā, and in the hymn in the *Harivaṁśa*, in which she is addressed as *Āryā*, the same epithets are applied to her. From the time of the *Mārkaṇḍeya Purāṇa*, Jayā and Vijayā are the names of Chaṇḍī's chief maids. Clearly *Vijayā*, originally, had no relation to the fight with Mahisha, whatever the idea may have been. *Jayā and Vijayā* differ no more than Victrix and Victoria. How the festival got its name, I do not know.'

left her mountain home, and whose image now leaves the homes of the people, are sung; these are far fewer than Āgāmanī songs. What the festival means to Hindus is thus expressed by a leading article this year (1922) in the *Amṛitā Bāzār Patrikā*, the most popular nationalist paper in Bengal. 'The spirit of Bijayā [*i.e.* Vijayā] means the spirit of peace and goodwill. On the day the image of the Goddess Durgā is immersed, the Hindu is required to immerse all unkindly and uncharitable feelings. He meets relations and friends, and makes peace with enemies on this day; the custom of the country is for everyone to salute his elders, to bless youngers, and to embrace whoever comes across him. As man is a quarrelsome being, naturally more or less spiteful and selfish, he is enjoined to make an effort on this sacred day to forget and forgive and make peace even with his bitterest foés.

'Each day of the Pūjā is a day of sacrifice; for the way to resurrection lies through the Cross, the road to higher life lies through a sacrifice of the lower. The extent of our sacrifice is the measure of our spiritual uplift, and this self-immolation is necessary that the lower gross vehicle may be purified of its dross and transformed into a fit instrument of the Divine Energy. . . .

'Once a year, on the sacred Bijayā day, let us anticipate this final transformation of humanity [*i.e.* into holiness of life and heart]; let us forget our petty jealousies and antagonisms, and realise that we are one in the bosom of the Universal Mother in whom all things live, move and have their being!'

On the next new moon night, the Kālī-pūjā is held. The dualism which overlies Hindu monism is expressed in these two festivals; Durgā (Umā) represents the beneficent face of Nature, Kālī the maleficent; and they are associated respectively with the bright and dark phases of the moon. Kālī's ritual is more rigid, and, so far as we can discover, it is not lawful to offer her bloodless sacrifices.

The reader will note the resemblances between the

Bengali 'drama of coming and going' and song-cycles of other lands. One thinks of the chorus of *Canticles* giving notice of the imminence of the kingly lover's arrival; or of peasant songs of Greece and Italy. Village poets are still improvising new details or embroidering old ones on the tale of Umā's sorrowful life with her vagabond husband, of her mother's joy at receiving her, and her grief at losing her. Though the Durgā-cult has annexed this legend, it has very different roots. Umā has the breath of Himālayan snows about her—still more, has the fragrance of autumn harvest fields in her hair—while Kālī and Durgā, especially Kālī, are children of a fierce, savage imagination, nurtured in jungle fastnesses.

E. J. T.

ŚĀKTA SONGS

RĀMPRASĀD SEN

I. THE CHILD'S COMPLAINT OF HIS MOTHER'S NEGLECT

Tell me where I may stand, Mother Tārā.[1] I am alone, O Śaṅkarī.[2] A mother's love brings the father's with it. But the father who dallies with a stepmother,[3] vainly does his child look to him. If *you* forget all kindness, shall I go to my stepmother? If a stepmother take me in her lap, will my mind's disquiet cease?[4]

Prasād says: In our scriptures this is written. He that names your name, Mother, wins for reward a garland of bones, and robes in tatters.

II. SHE IS UTTERLY INDIFFERENT

Is motherhood then a mere word of the lips? Bringing forth does not make a mother, unless she can understand the griefs of her child.

[1] *Star*; a name of Kālī.

[2] Śaṅkarī: Wife of Śaṅkara ('He who does good,' Śiva).

[3] Literally, 'The father who holds a stepmother on his head.' The reference is to 'Śiva,' who, in the purāṇic mythology, broke the fall of the Ganges from heaven to earth, by receiving the flood on his matted hair. Ganges becomes also co-wife with Kālī. So Rāmprasād says: Śiva's affections wander and are divided, and the worshipper of Kālī cannot look to Kālī's lord for affection, which he has given elsewhere.

[4] There are variant readings of most of Rāmprasād's poems, for they have gone from mouth to mouth for a century and a half, long before they were printed. In this line, we have taken the most intelligible reading.

Ten months and ten days a mother endures sorrow. But now, though I am hungry, my Mother does not ask where her child is. Earthly parents correct their sons, when they have offended.

Though you see Death, that dreadful ogre, coming to slay me, you are untroubled.

Twice-born[1] Rāmprasād says: Where did you learn this conduct? If you behave like your father,[2] do not take upon yourself the name of World-Mother.

III. HE WILL TURN TO HIS STEPMOTHER, SINCE HIS MOTHER IS APPARENTLY DEAD

Mind, call no longer Mother. You will not find her. Had she been alive, she would have come. But she is dead, and lives no longer.

Now go to your stepmother's bank; there burn an image of *kuśa*-grass; when the time of mourning has finished, leave on the bank your lump of rice. Then let us go to Kāśī.[3]

[1] A member of the higher castes, the three that are 'twice born,' Brahmins, Kshatriyas and Vaiśyas.

[2] Himālaya. The reader will find Rāmprasād frequently taunting his goddess with being stony by origin and stony by nature. Umā or Parvatī, child of Himālaya, is identified with Kālī and Durgā.

[3] In despair, he threatens to turn to the popular religion of ceremonial and pilgrimage, which he has so often scoffed at as useless. Ganges in Rāmprasād stands for this religion. Since his Mother Kālī is dead, he will perform the *Śrāddha* ceremony for her. This includes an offering of a lump of rice (piṇḍa) to the departed spirit, after the first period of mourning, which lasts (in the case of Brahmins) for ten days. The *Śrāddha* rites are partly ordinary funeral ones, partly those of ancestor-worship. The eldest son must perform them, which is why it is of such importance to Hindus to have a son.

When a person has been untraced for twelve years, his death is assumed, and, since his body is not available for the pyre, an image of *kuśa*-grass (Poa cynosuroides) is burnt.

IV. HIS MOTHER IS HIS ONLY HOPE

Give me freedom, Mother, whose locks are free. In the world, day and night I have sorrow. Queen, you have forgotten me, and left me in the Hand of Time.[1] O Tārā, when will this dreadful noose of Time be snapped?

Rāmprasād says: What will it avail, to go and live at Kāśī? My father, he who holds my stepmother on his head, has become a dweller in the burning ground.[2]

V. HE WILL ENDURE HER TRICKS OF DECEPTION NO LONGER

I see, Mother, how you are about to give me the slip! In this child's hand is no sweetmeat for you to snatch and eat.[3] I will so hide myself, Mother, that with all your search you will not find me. You will have to run after me, as a cow after her calf.

Rāmprasād says: The mother whose child is a fool can play tricks upon it. But if you, Mother, do not save me, may Śiva become your father.[4]

VI. HER NEGLECT OF HUMBLE WORSHIPPERS AND HER PARTIALITY FOR THE VIOLENT

Go, Mother, go! I know you. He that praises you gets double punishment. He that follows after you, with prayer and worship crying ever *Mother*, you send him with grief and pain and sorrow to the House of Yamā.[5]

[1] The word also means *Death*.

[2] Kāśī (Benares) is Śiva's seat. But Śiva has wandered away to the burning-grounds.

The uselessness of going to Kāśī is a favourite theme of Rāmprasād.

[3] *I.e.* to deceive him is not so simple as robbing a child and running off.

[4] This curious phrase is merely a coarse jibe.

[5] King of the Dead.

With little effort can anything come? The water flows past the weak embankment.[1] But he that is strong wins freedom by violence, freedom in his triple life.[2] Unless one actually thrusts his finger in your eyes, Mother, you never see, never judge.

Feet that Śiva longs for, these in your fear you have given to Mahishāsura![3] He who holds a sword can make you hear him! Fearing for your life, you have become his everlasting refuge.

Rāmprasād will be satisfied if he but win your grace. Leaving aside the Nine Senses,[4] worship the Feet of Śyāmā.[5]

VII. THE WORSHIPPER COMPLAINS OF THE INEQUALITY OF LOTS

Let us have a word or two about the problem of suffering. Let us talk about suffering, Tārā, let me express my mind.

Some say that you are humble and full of kindness.

Yes, Mother, to some you have given wealth, horses, elephants, charioteers, conquest. And the lot of others is field labour, with rice and vegetables.

[1] Embankments are of first-rate importance in Bengal, where all agriculture depends on three months of rain.

[2] Past, present and future.

[3] A demon killed by Durgā. As punishment for sin he was born as a demon; his sin was expiated when he was slain, and thus by his death at Durgā's hands salvation came to him.

Durgā is often represented as standing on Mahishāsura's body. Rāmprasād, by a rather weak conceit, taunts her with fearing the demon and therefore giving him her sacred feet (literally, by standing on his corpse) and so, salvation ('You have become his everlasting refuge').

[4] The *Nine Senses*: There are *Ten Senses*, five sensory and five motor organs. Rāmprasād means that he will leave the use of all but the organ of articulation; he will become a mere voice to praise the Mother.

[5] Śyāmā, the Dark Goddess.

Some live in palaces, as I myself would like to do. O Mother, are these fortunate folk your grandfathers,[1] and I no relation at all?

Some wear shawls and comfortable wrappers,[2] they have sugar and curds as well as rice.

Some ride in *pālkis*,[3] while I have the privilege of carrying them.

Mother, through what grain land of yours have I driven my plough?[4]

Prasād says: If I forget you, I endure the burden of grief that burns. Mother, my desire is to become the dust of those Feet that banish fear.

VIII. KĀLĪ'S SERVICE HAS MADE HIM A MENDICANT

No longer shall I call you Mother: countless ills have you sent me, Mother, countless ills are sending. I had home and dear ones, but you have made me a mendicant.[5] What worse can you do, O Long-Tressed Goddess?

I must go from door to door, begging my food. Even though the mother dies, does not the child live still? *Mother*, I cry, and yet again, *Mother*, but you are deaf and blind. While the mother lives, if the child suffers so, what is the use of his mother to him?

Rāmprasād says: Is this a mother's way—being the mother, to be her child's foe? Day and night I muse,

[1] Naturally the most honoured in a society whose inner sanctities are those of immediate ancestor-worship.

[2] A kind of shawl, in itself a luxury.

[3] Palanquins.

[4] The worst of offences in an agricultural country.

The commonest form of this poem is much briefer, bitterer, though less elaborately sarcastic:

'Well do I know thy kindness, ah! too well! Some go hungry after the day's toil; others carry rice in their belly, gold in their shoulder-cloth. Some ride in *pālkis*, others take the *pālki*-poles upon their shoulders. Some wear costly shawls, others rags and tatters.'

[5] *Sannyāsī*: He is said to have practically become one in his last years.

what shall I do? You will make me endure the pangs of birth again and again.[1]

A very famous song. There are variant readings.

IX. HIS DAYS ARE PASSED IN MISERY

In what have I offended so?

Unendurable has my daily lot become, all day I sit and weep. Inwardly I say, I will leave my home, I will dwell no longer in such a land. But the Wheel of Life turns me in its circle, and Chintārām *Chāprāsi*[2] awaits me. I say, I will leave my home, and pass my days praising the Name. But you, Kālī, have so wrought that I am bound fast to this vain show of things.

Weeping at Kālī's Feet, poor Rāmprasād says: This Kālī of mine, this Kālī of my thought,[3] through her I have become wretched.

X. THE VANITY OF LIFE AFTER LIFE

It is just the hope of hope, this coming into the world, and it all ends in coming,[4] the black bee's mistake when he falls on the pictured lotus. You have fed me with *nim*-leaves,[5] calling them sugar, deceiving me with words. Mother, in my greed for sweets, I have spent my whole day with wry, embittered lips.

[1] He desires to be set free from the cycle of re-births. The reference in this last line is to the belief that during the pre-natal period the child suffers intensely in the womb.

[2] A very homely, almost humorous, touch. Chintārām ('Lord of Anxiety') is Yama (Death); and Rāmprasād pictures him waiting like a *Chāprāsi* (servant in livery), to tell the man he is wanted elsewhere.

[3] The Bengali has a series of puns on Kālī and Kālā (*black*).

[4] A line of puns, on *āsā*, *coming*, and *āśā*, *hope* (different spelling, but similar sound).

[5] Which are very bitter. The *nim* is *Azidirachta indica*.

Mother, you brought me down into the world, saying, 'Let us play.'[1] You cheated me, and in the game that you have played my hope has not found fulfilment.

Rāmprasād says: In the world-play, what was to be has been. Now at eventide, taking your child in your bosom, go home.

Another famous song. The 'hope of hope' recalls the Greek σκιᾶς ὄναρ. Birth after birth, and all is vanity and disappointment.

XI. HE TRUSTS KĀLĪ THOUGH SHE NEGLECTS HIM

Mother, you are in my heart.

Dark Goddess, who says you are in my heart? You are a stony-hearted girl, a harmful delusion. Through how much trouble you make me pass! In the difference[2] of worship, all the Five Forms become yours. He that knows the Five are but One, from him, Mother, how will you escape? He that knows, and rests all on you, him you will not help! But will the man who knows the worth of gold accept glass?[3] Prasād says: My heart is of the right tint of the lotus.[4] You, building those five into one, dance and dwell in my mind!

XII. HIS VAIN AND EARNEST SEARCH FOR SALVATION BY KNOWLEDGE

I thought I had attained to truth. I had learnt from the wise. I found a teacher in the land where there is

[1] The reader will remember that to the Hindu all life is *līlā*, *sport* or *drama*.

[2] There are *Five* main cults, according to the deities worshipped (Siva, Kālī, Vishṇu, Sūrya—the Sun-God—and Gaṇeśa). All five cults, Rāmprasād says, are cults of the Mother, and she meets her worshippers in these five ways.

[3] Will he worship any other deity?

[4] 'Is five pure lotuses'—*i.e.* all the *Five* cults find a place in his heart. The Tantric system of physiology teaches that there

no night. My day and dusk alike I robbed of dusk. Sleep has gone. Shall I sleep again? Through all ages I remain awake. I will restore sleep to whatever owner claims it; I have put sleep itself to sleep. Mingling borax and sulphur,[1] I have brought out the glowing tint of gold.[2] This is my hope, to cleanse the temple of my mind.

Prasād says: Worship and salvation both I despise. The Dark Queen's name I know for God Supreme, and faith and works alike I abandon.

XIII. HE WOULD BE ACCEPTED FOR SERVICE

Appoint me your treasurer, Mother, and trust me. I am not one who forgets the salt he has eaten.

Everyone loots your storehouse of gems,[3] I cannot endure it. You have left it in charge of the Demon's Bane, Śiva the Forgetful.[4] He is swift to give, easy in complaisance, yet you let him keep your treasury! Half of you he has received as a fief;[5] then why pay him salary as well, and *such* salary? I, your wageless servant, possess but the dust of your Feet. If you be like your

are six circles (*chakras*) of occult force in the body; each of these is called a lotus.

[1] As goldsmiths do.

[2] 'I have painted the lily and gilded refined gold.' He is waxing sarcastic over his attainments and wisdom, before he flings them aside for ever, and abandons 'works' for 'faith' (or, rather, ecstatic devotion, *bhakti*).

[3] Literally, 'the gem-storehouse of your Feet.'

[4] She stands on Śiva, who in that way possesses her Feet. This possession is also the 'salary' which Śiva receives.

Śiva is 'the Forgetful,' lost in meditation, drowsed with drugs. *Śākta* poets indulge in a great deal of what must be called pious badinage of Śiva.

[5] In the combined image, half-Umā, half-Śiva, called Hara-Gaurī.

father,[1] I am lost. But, if you be like mine,[2] I shall grow wealthy.

Prasād says: Let me die in the saving grace of those Feet that spurn aside all forms of curse. If I may clasp those Feet,[3] all danger leaves me.

Traditionally, his first song, the one his employer found written in an account-book.

XIV. MEDICINE FOR HIS MIND'S DISEASE

My Mind, if you would only take my prescription! Here are *paṭals*[4] of truth, here is Śrīnāth Datta.[5]

The time will come when you will wish for these.

Forget your worldly bliss, and worship the Victor of Death![6]

Rāmprasād says: Then, my Mind, you will be healed from the world that is your disease.

The only interest of this poor but undoubtedly authentic song is that it is one of the few in which Rāmprasād draws on his hereditary medical lore, as a member of the *Vaidya* or doctor caste.

[1] See note to II. Rāmprasād means: If you are stony and hard-hearted, I shall get nothing.

[2] Śiva, the careless and generous; Rāmprasād's father by a kind of adoption, since the poet is child of Kālī, his consort.

[3] *Pada* means both *foot* and *post, employment*. Hence, the words mean also, if I may get this position.

[4] The *paṭal* is a vegetable. Vegetables are much used in prescriptions of *kavirājas*, or country doctors.

[5] Śrīnāth Datta seems to have been Rāmprasād's spiritual preceptor.

[6] Mṛituñjaya, a name of Śiva. There seems to be only one place—in the *Purāṇas*—where an explanation of the name is attempted; and that explanation is too obscure to be given here. It is sufficient to remember that Śiva is the Great Destruction that itself cannot be destroyed.

XV. THE FOOLISHNESS OF PILGRIMAGE

What have I to do with Kāśī? The Lotus-Feet of Kālī are places of pilgrimage enough for me. Deep in my heart's lily[1] meditating on them, I float in an ocean of bliss. In Kālī's name where is there place for sin? When the head is not, headache cannot remain.[2] As when fire consumes a heap of cotton, so all goes in Kālī's name.

The worshipper of Kālī laughs at the name of Gayā,[3] and at ancestral offerings there and the story of salvation by ancestors' merits. Certainly, Śiva has said[4] that if a man dies at Kāśī he wins salvation. But devotion is the root of everything, and salvation but her handmaid who follows her. What is the worth of salvation if it means absorption, the mixing of water with water? Sugar I love to eat, but I have no wish to become sugar.

Prasād says joyously: By the power of grace and mercy, if we but think on the Wild-locked Goddess, the Four Goods[5] become ours.

The teaching and spirit of this poem are Vaishṇava, rather than Śākta.

XVI. THE HOLINESS OF KĀŚI EXPLAINED

What need for me to go to Kāśī? Upon the breast of Kāśī's maker[6] is Kālī with her flowing locks. Men

[1] The fourth 'lotus' or centre of occult power. See note to No. XI.

[2] The very root and source of all sin is destroyed.

[3] Śrāddha ceremonies for one's deceased relatives are held to bring far more religious merit if performed at Gayā than at any other place. Here Gautama the Buddha attained enlightenment, and here Krishna is said to have killed Gayāsura.

[4] In the *Tantras*, where he is the speaker.

[5] *The Four Ends* or *Objects of Pursuit: Dharma* (religious merit or duty), *Artha* (wealth), *Kāma* (physical desire), and *Mōksha* (liberation of the spirit from bondage).

[6] Śiva. In Hindu Mythology Śiva upholds the place on his trident.

have proclaimed its name as Maṇikarṇi,[1] for there it was that Jagadambā's[2] ear-ring fell from her. Between the Asi and the Varuṇā[3] stands Benares the sacred. The stream of the Varuṇā is the stream of the Mother's mercy, and the Asi is the stream of blood from the sword.[4] If one dies at Kāśī, Śiva gives him the knowledge of truth.[5] Above that knowledge is enthroned Maheśa's[6] Queen.

Rāmprasād: What care I for going to Kāśī? See around my neck as garland I have bound the name of Kālī.

XVII. HE SOMETIMES LONGS TO REST AT KĀŚĪ

When shall I be a dweller in Kāśī? When look back on sorrow from those groves of gladness? With Ganges water and with leaves of *bel*,[7] I will worship Śiva my lord. Whether on water or on land it matters

[1] 'A gem of the ear'—the name of a pool at Kāśī. Daksha, son of Brahmā the Creator, was father-in-law of Śiva, who had married his daughter Satī. Offended by his son-in-law's absent-minded neglect to show him reverence, he excluded Śiva from a sacrifice to which all the other gods were invited. Satī came, though in the invitations passed over with her husband; and, overcome with shame at her father's contempt of herself and her husband, died in her father's sacrificial fire, thus becoming the first *satī* or 'faithful wife.' Śiva carried her body about, in mad dance threatening all things with destruction. Vishṇu cut Satī's body to pieces, whereupon Śiva's frenzy subsided. Satī's ear-rings fell in the Maṇikarṇi pool at Kāśī. Satī was reborn as Umā, and is therefore identified with Kālī and Durgā.

[2] 'Mother of the world' (Kālī).

[3] Two mythical rivers supposed to be on either side of Benares. Rāmprasād explains them allegorically.

[4] *I.e.* of sacrifice.

[5] *Tat tam asi, Thou art that*, the master-word of the Upanishads.

[6] *The Great God* (Śiva).

[7] *Aegle marmelos*, sacred to Śiva and Śakti (Kālī). It is the rule to offer a *tripatra*, *i.e.* three *bel* leaves on a single stalk.

not, only let me die away there at Benares and salvation will be mine. She who feeds the world[1] is there as queen, that golden one in whom I will take refuge. Then will I dance, and, striking my cheek, shout '*Bam*,[2] *Bam*, *Bhōlā*.'

This poem may serve as a contrast to the preceding. It shows Rāmprasād as in some moods a conformist. But we are inclined to regard it as spurious.

XVIII. THE FOOLISHNESS OF SACRIFICE

Mind, why art thou so anxious? Utter Kālī's name, and sit in meditation. From all this pomp of worship the mind grows proud. Worship her in secret, that none may know. What is thy gain from images of metal, stone or earth?

Fashion her image with the stuff of mind, and set it on the lotus-throne of your heart. Parched rice and plantains, ah! how vainly do you offer these! Feed her with the nectar of devotion, and satisfy your own mind.

Why seek to illumine her with lamp and lantern and candle? Light the jewelled lamp of the mind, let it flash its lustre day and night.

Why do you bring sheep and goats and buffaloes for sacrifice? Saying 'Victory to Kālī,' 'Victory to Kālī,' sacrifice the Six Passions.[3]

[1] Annapurṇā, a name of Durgā.

[2] Pronounce 'Bom,' as the *a* is the included vowel which every consonant carries. The cry of Śiva and of those ascetics who serve him. Bhōlā is short for Bhōlānātha, 'Lord of Forgetfulness.'

[3] The Six Passions are—*Kāma* or Sexual Appetite, *Krōdha* or Anger, *Lōbha* or Covetousness, *Mōha* (literally, Stupefaction) or Lapse or Aberration due to Infatuation, *Mada* or Pride, *Mātsarya* or Envy. Cf. the *Seven Deadly Sins* of the Middle Ages.

Prasād says: What need is there of drums and tomtoms? Saying, 'Victory to Kālī,' clap your hands and lay your mind at her Feet.

Another famous song, of which variant texts exist.

XIX. THE SOUL'S SLEEP OF DEATH

Drowsy with desire, you wake not. Excellent is this bed of time[1] that you have found! Think you there will never be any dawn from this night of happiness? Desire sits in your lap like a harlot, and you will not turn from her. You have drawn the sheet of hope over your body; muffling up your face, you refuse to uncover. Winter and summer alike, you remain thus, and your filthy cloth you never send to the wash. You have drunk the wine of worldly possessions and the stupor of that wine holds you down. Day and night a drunkard, even in absent-mindedness, you do not utter Kālī's name.

O you foolish Prasād, foolish beyond conception, even thus your sleep hunger is not appeased. In this your sleep the great sleep will come, when you will not wake,[2] though we call and call.

Another famous song.

XX. HE IS OLD, DEPENDENT AND DESPISED

By time's passing I have lost my work. The day is spent in idle joyfulness. When I earned money, I wandered freely from place to place. Then I had

[1] *Time*, remember, means also *Death*.

[2] The words mean more: when you will not awake to consciousness of any kind.

friends, brothers, wife, and all these heeded my wishes; but now all that is over, for I am no more a wage-winner. Those friends and brothers, wife and children, seeing me penniless, scold and grow wrathful. When Death's Messenger, seated by my pillow, makes ready to grip me by the hair, then, preparing my bier of wood, my pitcher of water,[1] and my shroud, they will bid farewell to the man in the ascetic's garb. Shouting Hari,[2] Hari, they will fling me on the pile, and each go his way. Rāmprasād is dead, the weeping is done, and they will fall to their meal quite cheerfully.[3]

This and the next are very popular songs.

XXI. THE USELESS TOIL OF HIS DAYS

I perish, slaving like a brownie.[4] My waistcloth is empty of money for my journey; I am become a public drudge, vainly working myself to death. Day by day, I labour like a coolie, Mother; and the Five Elements divide the wage of one.[5] The Five Elements, the Six Passions, the Ten Senses, stand like bullies,[6] bearing clubs. They listen to no one. My days pass in toil. As a blind man grips his stick that he lost and has found again, so would I fain clasp thee, elusive Mother; but in my evil deeds thou fleest from me.

[1] Friends pour pitchers of water on the ashes, after the corpse has been burned.

[2] A name of Vishṇu; the funeral-cry in Bengal.

[3] 'Easily'; as a matter of course.

[4] *Bhūta, evil spirit*, or *ghost*. Our rendering will throw back the reader's mind to Milton's 'lubber fiend' (*L'Allegro*). Cf. No. LIII.

[5] I am not master in my own house. I slave for the benefit of these my five material constituents. (See note 8 on No. XLVI.) The Five Elements are compared to a Hindu joint family, all employed battening (as sometimes happens) on what is earned by the only member.

[6] *Lāṭhiāls*, hired ruffians.

Prasād says: Mighty Mother, cut asunder this rope of actions.[1] When death draws nigh, Mother, grant that my life may burst its way out through my head.[2]

XXII. THE TYRANNY OF A DIVIDED WILL

Mother, how often shall I make my complaint to thee?

I am floating like weeds in a sea of misery. I am without root and without station or direction. Six several ways the Six Passions pull me, and sorely hurt I fall in the midst of them.

Twice-born Rāmprasād says: Mother, now I know that you are without mercy. Fulfil this life of mine by granting me vision once of thee standing in my temple.

XXIII. KĀLĪ NEGLECTS HER WORSHIPPER, IN MAD DANCE

All this is a girl's madcap pleasure, in whose enchantment the three worlds swoon into forgetfulness. She is mad, her lord is mad, his two disciples[3] are mad. Her beauty and her nature, her gestures and her thought, surpass all speech. If one takes her name, one's happiness flames into ashes,[4]

[1] He wishes to escape from the round of rebirth, due to actions.

[2] Through the *Brahmarandhra*, the hole for the *Brahman*, just above the foramen of Monro. It is believed that, if the vital breath goes out at death through this hole, the soul goes direct to the World (Abode) of Brahman, from which there is no returning to the Cycle of Births and Deaths.

[3] Nandī and Bhriṅgī, two faithful demons, who attend on Śiva; comic characters, but mischievous and powerful, and ruthless in execution of his orders.

[4] Literally, 'the forehead is burnt,' an extremely common expression. It is believed that the sutures of the front of the skull are a man's written fate. 'It is worse than vain, it is misery to worship so careless a goddess.'

and the burning pain of poison comes into the throat.[1]

XXIV. KĀLĪ THE BATTLE-QUEEN

Ever art thou dancing in battle, Mother. Never was beauty like thine, as, with thy hair flowing about thee, thou dost ever dance, a naked warrior on the breast of Śiva.[2]

Heads of thy sons, daily freshly killed, hang as a garland around thy neck. How is thy waist adorned with human hands! little children are thy ear-rings. Faultless are thy lovely lips; thy teeth are fair as the *kunda*[3] in full bloom. Thy face is bright as the lotus-flower, and terrible is its constant smiling. Beautiful as the rain-clouds is thy form; all blood-stained are thy Feet.

Prasād says: My mind is as one that dances. No longer can my eyes behold such beauty.

XXV. ŚIVA UNDER KĀLĪ'S FEET

Come down from Hara's[4] breast and dance no more, you mad old hag.

Śiva is not dead, he is alive; he, the great saint, is lost in meditation.

Such is the strength of those feet of yours that with your dancing you will break Bhōlā's ribs.

[1] Śiva drank the poison which came out when the gods and giants churned the ocean and which threatened all lives. Hence his throat became stained blue, and he was Nīlakaṇṭha, *blue-throated*.

[2] Kālī is usually represented standing on Śiva's body. After slaying the demon Mahishāsura she danced, shaking the world. In her excitement she ignored even her husband's request that she should stop. So he lay down; and, when she found herself on his body, she thrust out her tongue in dismay. Rāmprasād in some poems takes this story symbolically; Kālī is over Śiva, is greater than he.

[3] A jasmine.

[4] 'He who takes away, who destroys,' *i.e.* Śiva.

Śiva, you know, has swallowed poison[1] and so his strength has gone.

Come down, and do your dancing, Mother, you who are loved by Śiva. He whom the poison could not kill, why should he die today?

Says Rāmprasād: He is feigning death that he may possess your bloodstained Feet.

XXVI. THE STORM-PROCESSION OF ŚIVA

Jagadambā's watchmen go out into dread, black night, Jagadambā's watchmen! 'Victory! Victory to Kālī!' they cry, and, clapping their hands and striking upon their cheeks, they shout *Bam*, *Bam*. That worshippers may tremble, the flowery chariot is in the sky and in it rides the ghosts, in it too are *bhairavas* and *vetālas*.[2] Upon their heads is the half-moon crest,[3] in their hands the dreadful trident; to their feet hangs down their matted hair. With them first come the serpents strong as death, then follow mighty tigers, monstrous bears. They roll their red eyes before the worshippers, who, half-dead with fear, cry out, no longer able to sit at their devotions.

Can aught evil befall the true worshipper? Rather in his delight he finds all things are good. By the power of that Dread-visaged one,[4] thy prayers are made effectual, thou dost conquer both in this life and the next.

[1] See note to XXIII.

[2] Ghosts (*bhūtas*) are ordinary sinful spirits; *Bhairava* (*the terrible one*) is a name of Śiva, but is also used for his lieutenants who command the demon-world under him; *vetālas* are the spirits of people who have died by accident or by suicide, without having completed their allotted term.

[3] Chandra the Moon was husband of the twenty-seven stars of the Hindu zodiac, the daughters of Daksha. He neglected them all for one of them, Rōhiṇī. The twenty-six complained to their father, who laid on the Moon the curse that he should waste away. The Moon besought Śiva's aid; and he wears the crescent moon always, lest the Moon fade out of existence.

[4] Kālī.

Rāmprasād, a poet and her slave, is swimming in a sea of happiness. Can misfortune come to one who worships? What cares he for these dread things? He sits *vīrāsana*[1] at his devotions and takes the name of Kālī as his shield.

XXVII. THE WORSHIPPER'S HEART IS KĀLĪ'S HOME

The Happy One is in my heart; ever is she playing there. I meditate on thoughts that come to me, but never do I forget her name. Though both my eyes are closed, yet in my heart I see her, garlanded with heads of men.

Possessions, understanding, all are gone, and men say I am mad. Let them say what they will; but at last, I pray thee, spurn me not.

Rāmprasād says: Present art thou within my lotus-heart.[2] Spurn me not at the last, Mother, me who have found refuge at thy Feet.

XXVIII. NEGLECTED OPPORTUNITY

Mind, thou dost not know how to farm. Thy fields remain untilled; hadst thou sown, a golden harvest had waved. Now make of Kālī's name a fence, that the yield may not be destroyed. Not Death himself[3] (O my Mind!) dare come nigh this fence, thy long-haired[4]

[1] *Vīrāsana*, 'the hero-seat,' with *both* legs crossed, the right foot above the left thigh, the left foot above the right thigh. One of the attitudes prescribed for meditation to the followers of the *yōga* philosophy. The *Śākta* authorities variously estimate the number of these attitudes, from eighty-four to eight million four hundred thousand. Practically any Hindu can adopt the *vīrāsana* attitude; but the translators, both accustomed to English athletic exercises all their lives, cannot manage it.

[2] See notes to XI and XV.

[3] Yama, who comes, like Hermes, for the souls that are his.

[4] Literally, 'She whose tresses are free.' Rāmprasād makes frequent play of fancy with the wild locks of Kālī, seeing in them the symbol of strength in freedom. In this passage, as in so many, there is a play on words that does not admit of translation.

Fortress. Today or after a hundred centuries, thou knowest not when forfeiture[1] will come. Lo, to thy hand is the present time, Mind (O my Mind!). Ah, haste and gather harvest! Scatter now the seed thy teachers gave thee, and sprinkle it with the water of love.[2]

And if alone (O my mind!) thou canst not do this, then take Rāmprasād with thee.[3]

XXIX. THE TYRANNY OF REBIRTH

Mother, how often will you drive me round and round the Wheel of Being, like a blindfold ox that grinds the oil? Binding me to the log of the world, you urge me round incessantly. For what guilt have you subjected me to six oilmen?[4] After wandering through eighty *lākhs*[5] of rebirths, in form of beast and bird, still the door of the womb is not closed to me, but sorely hurt I come again. When the child weeps, uttering the dear name of Mother, then the mother takes it in her lap. Throughout the whole world I see this comes to pass, I alone am excepted. Crying Durgā, many sinners have attained to pardon.

Take this binding from my eyes, that I may see the Feet which banish fear. Countless are the evil children, but who ever heard of an evil mother?

Mother, this is the hope of Rāmprasād, that at the end I may find station at your Feet.

Another well-known song.

'(She) thy free-tressed, strong fence,' where the word for *strong*, *śākta*—is the same root as Kālī's name of *Śakti*. She, the Emancipated One, is Strength, says Rāmprasād; and there is no defence like freedom. *Durga* is a fortress, Durgā is the goddess.

[1] Forfeiture—of life.

[2] *Bhakti*—passionate, ecstatic devotion.

[3] Throughout this poem, the 'Mind' represents the desiring part, wandering and ineffective. Take all I am, says the poet; and use the body as your servant, to accomplish your will. Even so, Francis of Assisi would speak of his body as 'Brother Ass,' the drudge of his will and mind.

[4] The Six Passions.

[5] A *lākh* is 100,000.

XXX. STRENGTH WITHIN ONESELF

Crying Kālī's name, plunge deep, my Mind, down in the unfathomed shining sea of thy heart. Never empty of gems is that sea, though diving twice or thrice thou gainest nought. Conquer thy passionate heart,[1] and plunge! Make way to the very depths of the essential well that is thyself![2] In the Waters of Knowledge fruits the Pearl of Strength,[3] my Mind! By devotion[4] thou shalt obtain it, if thou keep the word of Śiva in memory.[5]

Like crocodiles, the Six Passions lurk greedy for prey, they wander ever. Smear thy body with the ochre of good conscience,[6] the scent will keep them far from thee.

Countless gems and jewels lie in those waters!

[1] Holding the breath, as divers do. There is also a reference to the *Yōga* philosophy, which enjoins the practice of suppressing breathing, as an aid to escape from the body's thraldom.

[2] Literally, '(Holding thy breath) dive to the side of Kulakuṇḍalinī.' Kulakuṇḍalinī is Śakti seated in the Mūlādhāra (the first 'lotus'—above the rectum, below the sacro-coccygeal plexus), coiled up like a serpent in three-and-a-half spirals. The devotee awakens this Śakti from sleep and draws her up through the *Sushumṇā* (the central passage of the spinal cord) and enjoys Divine Bliss; for this Śakti is she who dances the Eternal Dance and is the Source (or Giver) of Bliss (Ānanda). The puzzled Western reader may recollect how strangely physical were many of our European metaphysical and psychological theories, with their fanciful locations of feelings and passions in this and that organ. The Indian *Yōga* philosophy emphasises this essential truth, that concentration of thought is needed, to worship and find God; but some of the physical methods by which it teaches us to attain that concentration are based on grotesque theories of physiology and lead to suppression of vitality and to semi-imbecility.

[3] The Pearl of *Śakti* (Kālī).

[4] *Bhakti*.

[5] If he follows the Tāntric discipline (Śiva is the speaker in the *Tantras*).

[6] Turmeric, smeared on the body, is supposed to keep off crocodiles. Rāmprasād means, 'Adopt the yellow robes of an ascetic and all passions will leave you.'

Rāmprasād says: Leap in, and thou shalt gather gems in heaps.

A difficult poem, crammed with allusion and conceit and with reference to Purāṇic mythology, Tantric teaching and folklore.

XXXI. THE UNGUARDED HOUSE

Wake and watch and cry, my Mind, Victory to Kālī! Give not way to sleep, forgetful Mind, to lose your treasure. When you lie in the senseless ease of sleep, in the House of Nine Doors,[1] then with slumber the robber will come, will pierce through the wall and bear your jewels away.

XXXII. THE STORM-SMITTEN HOUSE

I live in a damaged house, my Mother, so in my fear it is to thee that I cry. The tempests have blown it down, but Kālī's name sustained it. Terrified am I of those Six Thieves that at night come leaping over the mud wall.

A poem which, as well as any, shows how close to the soil Rāmprasād's thought and inspiration are. The village houses are of mud and suffer terribly in the Rains.

XXXIII. PERIL OF TEMPEST

Mind of mine, why art thou so afraid? Why, O why, art thou so afraid? When thou seest the tempest, have no fear, for tempest it is not. Embark in Durgā's name and sail away. If, as thou goest, the watch-

[1] The Body. The Nine Doors are the nine physical outlets or inlets.

man[1] sayeth aught to thee, then cry to him that thou art child of Śyāmā, thy Mother.

Prasād says: O mind beside thyself, whom dost thou fear? My body I have sold to Dakshiṇā,[2] a slave to her service.

XXXIV. THE MIND'S BOATMEN ARE CRAVEN

Beware, beware, the boat is sinking!

Ah, my careless mind, the days are passing, and thou hast not worshipped the Queen of Ruin.[3] Thou hast weighed down thy boat with vain goods of thy traffic, thy buying and selling. All day thou hast waited at the *ghāt*, and now with evening thou wouldst cross the stream.[4] Thou hast made thine old boat heavy with sins. If thou wouldst pass over the ocean of the world, make the Lord[5] thy helmsman. Seeing the leaping waves, the Six Boatmen[6] have fled. Mind, now trust thine all with thy teacher,[7] he will be thy helmsman.

XXXV. THE WORSHIPPER'S CASE COMES TO COURT

This is the usual judgment of the Mother! For the one who day and night calls upon Durgā's name misfortune is decreed.

[1] *Chaukidār*, the village watchman. This class of men have a bad reputation. The *chaukidār* might try to stop Rāmprasād, in hope of a bribe.

[2] 'The favourable one' (Kālī). The word literally means 'of the south,' the region from which spring breezes come.

[3] 'Queen of Hara' ('He who takes away').

[4] To the Hindu, life is more often a river than a road, and salvation is a ferrying across the stream of the world.

[5] Śrīnāth; literally, Lord of Śrī or Lakshmī (*i.e.* Vishṇu). But Rāmprasād almost certainly means 'Trust—and obey—your spiritual guide, Śrīnāth (Datta).' The teacher is idealised into a revelation, almost an incarnation, of the Deity.

[6] The Five 'Senses' of seeing, hearing, smelling, tasting and feeling; *and* the Mind. All of them are distinguished from the *Ātman* or soul. The boat is the body, the organic vehicle of the soul.

[7] Literally, 'Thy teacher-Brahmā'; 'Thy teacher-god.'

Within thine august presence, Mother, I am come, and stand with folded hands[1] before thee. When will my case be heard, that I may be freed from my dilemma?

What answers can I give to questionings? No understanding is there in this earthen pot.[2] Mother, my single hope is in the word of Śiva, which is one with what the Vedas and Āgamas[3] have declared.

Rāmprasād says: Mother, through fear of death I would escape and haste from here. So may, I, with my latest breath call upon Durgā's name, and on the banks of Jāhnavī's[4] stream forsake this earthly life!

The first of a group of poems which show that Bengali life was as full of litigation in the eighteenth century as it is today. They are packed with technical legal terms.

XXXVI. HE WILL APPEAL TO ŚIVA

No weakling, child untimely-born,[5] am I, O Tārā. Though angry eyes flash fire at me, I do not fear. Those bloodstained Feet that rest on Śiva's lotus-breast, in them is my prosperity. Mother, if I would look upon this wealth[6] of mine, what troubles must I endure! Yet is my title safe within my heart, a deed

[1] The attitude of an accused person in an Indian court.

[2] See p. 59, note 7. When the 'life-giving' ceremony of an idol takes place, the deity to whom it is dedicated is supposed to enter it. But a pot of water is placed beside the idol, for the reception of other deities than the one to whom the image belongs. Rāmprasād means that he is a pot that has failed to obtain the life-giving spirit.

[3] Another name for the *Tantras*.

[4] The Ganges. She interrupted the meditations of the Saint Jahnu, who drank up all waters, but discharged them again from his ear, when besought by the gods not to detain the holy stream. She is called Jāhnavī ('Jahnu's daughter').

[5] Literally, a child of the eighth month. A variant reading is, 'a child twenty-eight days old.'

[6] Kālī's feet.

that bears Śiva's signature and seal. Now will I make my plaint before my lord,[1] and I shall win the verdict[2] with one question.[3] When I appeal in court, then will I show what sort of child I am, and at the trial bring as evidence the deed my *guru* gave me.[4]

Says Rāmprasād: It is no paltry suit that I thy child would institute against thee, Mother, nor will I cease to urge my case till thou dost take me to thy arms and grant me peace.

XXXVII. HE HAS PAID ALL RENT DUES

Stand a moment, Death! Let me loudly invoke the Mother's name. Though thou wouldst take me with thee, yet am I unconcerned. Have I in vain bound round my neck as talisman the garland of Tārā's name?

Maheśwarī[5] is my landlord, I am her own immediate tenant. Now am I subject,[6] now am I free,[6] yet never have my dues to her been left unpaid.

Prasād says: Can others understand the drama[7] of the Mother's life? That which Trilōchan's[8] self

[1] Kālī is capricious, and he threatens to lodge a suit against her in Śiva's court.

[2] Rāmprasād uses the English word *decree*. It would be interesting to know if there is any earlier occurrence of an English word in a Bengali text. Clearly, this poem must be one of his latest, when the English law-courts were well established in Calcutta.

[3] Presumably, the question, 'Have you acted as your *guru* instructed you?'

[4] Every Hindu is supposed to have a spiritual preceptor, who teaches him *mantraṣ* or texts. Rāmprasād will show that he has received orthodox teaching. It will be remembered that Śrīnāth Datta was his preceptor.

[5] *The Great Goddess.*

[6] *Nātāna* and *Sātāna*, two East Bengal words, so rare today that very few know their meaning. A tenant who is *Sātāna* is one from whom his landlord demands gifts (in addition to rent); one who is *nātāna* can give only labour.

[7] Līlā, a word familiar to all students of Indian thought.

[8] Śiva, 'The three-eyed.' The reader will have noted how the *Śāktas* exalt Kālī at her lord's expense.

cannot perceive, shall such a mystery be vouchsafed to me?

XXXVIII. HIS MOTHER HAS NO LAWFUL CLAIMS AGAINST HIM

I am no fugitive from justice.

Of what, then, Mother, would you make me feel afraid?

My land agreement is outside your rent-roll,[1] Mother; the land I hold is also short in measurement;

And I hold, against rent-day, a talisman[2] sealed with a wondrous mystic word.

I am a tenant on the Mother's personal land,[3] keeping a firm hold of the right plot, all dues paid.

Now by the strength of your name, I mean to continue to hold it, and also to make it rent-free.[4]

Prasād says: My rent is not a single cowrie in arrears. You may sink me fathoms deep in sorrow; yet will I make my protest at your Feet.

XXXIX. SIN MUST BEAR ITS PUNISHMENT

Terribly afraid am I, my Mother. There with my judge are the records: credit and debit, all is written down. In former days I served my passions, nor cared what would befall me afterwards.

See yonder sits dread Chitragupta,[5] and whate'er I do he has registered.

[1] Temporary tenures were outside the permanent land-roll, in the days of the East India Company.

[2] The talisman, which bears as a seal the chief *mantra* of his faith, and which will save him from ruin when rent-day comes round, is his consciousness that he is a child of Kālī.

[3] This *khās jamī*, or personal land, falls outside the regular rent-roll.

[4] The payment of a lump sum, about 30 years' rent, can make land rent-free for ever.

[5] The Accountant of the Judge of the Dead.

From life to life he carries on the balance that is against me. Little have I saved, much have I spent. How can I escape the judgment of the king?

Within the mind of Rāmprasād the only hope is Kālī's name.

XL. HE IS BANKRUPT

Whom dost thou serve (O my Mind)? Who art thou? Who is thy master? Whose menial art thou? Thou must render an account of all thy folly; prepare to make the payment. O Mind, the income side is blank, I see; then borrow something for thy credit (O my Mind!).

The twice-born Rāmprasād says: The Name of Tārā is my wealth (O foolish one!), O Mind of-mine, why waste thy strength in profitless labour for wife and child?

XLI. PROSPERITY, THE SNARE OF THE SOUL

Mind, if you would rest in the shadow of safety, look not for happiness! Son of Virtue, leave your home; losing in the throw, seek the forest.[1] The Righteous Judge, the God of all Gods,[2] is a beggar and indigent, even because of what he is. He that is wretched loves mercy, my Mind, but the desire of pleasure breeds hardness. In bliss is teen, my Mind; let not this saying offend you. In joy is sorrow, in sorrow joy; this has been said by Ḍāk.[3]

You have thought to hide your greed of gain by insincere devotion. You will grasp every meanest coin, not a cowrie or a mote's weight will escape you!

[1] Yudhishṭhira (in the *Mahābhārata*) gambled and lost his kingdom, accepting loyally the issue of his risk.

[2] Śiva the Ascetic. He knows how valueless everything is.

[3] The traditional utterer of a number of proverbial sayings, *The Sayings of Ḍāk* (the twelfth century A.D. or earlier).

If you are Prasād's mind, why do you play a churl's part? Act like the mind you are, giving your strength fully; your reward shall be the jewel, the supremely excellent.

XLII. THE FEAR OF DEATH

My Mind, why so fretful, like a motherless child? Coming into the world you sit brooding, shivering in the dread of death. Yet there is a Death[1] that conquers death, the Mightiest Death, which lies beneath the Mother's Feet. You, a serpent, fearing frogs! How amazing! What terror of death is this in you, the child of the Mother-Heart of all? What folly is this, what utter madness? Child of that Mother-Heart, what will you dread? Wherefore brood in vain sorrow?

Utter without ceasing Durgā's name, as terror vanishes with waking, so will it be with you.

The twice-born Rāmprasād says: Mind, quit you like mind! Act the truth your teachers showed you. What then can the Child of the Sun[2] do unto you?

XLIII. LIFE'S FOURTH STAGE

Mother, tell me where to stand. I have no one here. Bidding good-bye to action,[3] I shall wander hither, thither. Joined with saints, in divers fashion I will banish my griefs of mind.

[1] Śiva the Destroyer. He has conquered death, being himself that Destruction in which all lesser destructions merge; yet it will be remembered that he is represented as lying beneath Kālī's feet, while she stands on his prostrate body.

[2] Yama, God of Death. In the Purāṇic mythology, he is child of the Sun.

[3] Life's four stages, in Hinduism, are: As Student, as Householder and Citizen, as Saint in Forest Meditation, as Wandering Mendicant. Rāmprasād means he will take up the fourth stage.

You are the daughter of the rocks, and my Mother is like my Father.[1]

Rāmprasād says: Keep in your heart your teacher's chain of wisdom.[2]

XLIV. HE IS POOR AND HELPLESS

Ever must I remain thus? Thou who art gracious to the lowly, what is to befall me? I am without deeds, without merit of worship, weak and poor inconceivably. Ah, wilt thou fulfil this my impossible wish? Shall I gain those Feet?

Whether I am an obedient child or disobedient, is not all known to those Feet? Though her child be disobedient, does the mother forsake it? To whom shall I speak all this?

Prasād has said: Except Tārā's, what other name is there I can take? Śiva has cherished this name in his heart.

XLV. HE IS A SLAVE IN HIS OWN HOUSE

Tārā, my Mother, listen to the story of my woe. Thou who art all supreme, behold this house of mine, how poor a thing it is.

Thus do these live, my Mother, with whom I share the house! Five[3] of them are there with five different wills, and all seek nothing but to please themselves.

Eight million houses[4] have I lived in heretofore, and now am come again to occupy the house of Man.

A fool's part do I play upon the stage of life, the cup of sorrow brimming over. That is reality for me, my Mother!

Heed then, O Mother, the word of Rāmprasād. My mind is not at rest. No longer would I live here in this

[1] Śiva, the careless and forgetful. Kālī (as Pārvatī, the Mountain-Queen) was daughter of Himālaya.

[2] Srīnāth Datta's teaching.

[3] The Five Senses. Again the joint-family inconvenience.

[4] In previous incarnations.

house; those six,[1] the masters of the house, have made an end of me.

XLVI. THE LIFE TO COME

Think awhile, Brothers, of what will be after death. This is the question that all debate.

Some say that thou wilt become a ghost,[2] some a restless shade;[3] some that we go to bliss,[4] some that we attain to where God dwells,[5] some that the soul is withdrawn into the Deity.[6]

Thou art the revelation of the Vedas; thou art the sky reflected in the earthen pot: death is but the shattering of the pot.[7] When all things are over, in the void our sins and virtue are weighed. Five are they who dwell in this one house;[8] and each, when time comes, will go to his own place.

[1] The Six Passions.

[2] *Bhūta*; a ghost, usually a malevolent spirit. See note to XXVI. The word is used also of the Five Elements that make up the body. See note 8 below.

[3] *Preta*; a ghost whose obsequies have not been performed, or the ghost of a deformed person. For an excellent account of the village demonology of the United Provinces, which resembles that of Bengal in general, see Briggs, *The Chamārs*, pp. 128-47. But *Bhūta preta* is used as a collective term, and the text here may not mean much more than 'we become ghosts and spectres'—*spectre* standing for the slightly more attenuated and less malevolent existence of a *preta*.

[4] *Swarga*; Indra's paradise.

[5] *Sālōkya*; 'dwelling in the same region with' (God).

[6] *Sāyujya*; 'union with' (God).

[7] The central doctrine of the Vedānta is the identity of the human and the divine spirit: Kālī, to Rāmprasād, is the divine spirit. The doctrine of identity is commonly illustrated by the reflection of the sky in the water in an earthen pot: it is the same sky you see, whether you look up or down. The phrase in the text, *ghaṭākāśa*, 'the sky in the earthen pot,' comes from Gauḍapāda's *Kārikās*, III, 4, and is frequently quoted. Hence 'earthen pot' is often used for the human body.

[8] *The Five Elements* (*bhūtas*); Earth, Water, Fire, Air and Ether. The body is supposed to be made up of them. They dissolve partnership at death.

Prasād says: What you were, Brother, you will become again at death; even as the bubbles that rise in water, becoming water, mix with water.

XLVII. KĀLĪ THE ONLY REFUGE

Mind, worship her who saves on the other side of the Ocean of the World.[1] Know once for all what worth is in the trash of wealth. Vain is hope in men or money, this was said of old time. Where wast thou, whence hast thou come, and whither, O whither, wilt thou go?

The world is glass,[2] and ever amid its snares delusion makes men dance. Thou art in the lap of an enchantress, held fast in thy prison. Pride, malice, anger, attachment to thy lovers, by what wisdom of judgment was it that thou didst divide the kingdom of thy body among these? The day is nearly done: think therefore in thy heart, the resting-place of Kālī, that island filled with jewels, think upon the things that day has brought thee.

Prasād says: The name of Durgā is my promised Land of Salvation, fields flowing with nectar. Tell thy tongue evermore to utter her name.

XLVIII. LIFE'S AFFLICTIONS

It is not over yet, not yet, this gloomy fate of mine. Not over yet, not yet! Ever is it passing, passing; but it does not pass. My mother's sister,[3] what a plague she is!

For me, I'd have a mind that's well content; that aunt of mine brings me sorrows manifold. Her snares delude me, Oh, what tricks they play me! A double portion of affliction does she bring me, and swells the sum of my adversities.

[1] The Ocean of Being; the Cycle of Births and Deaths.

[2] Brittle and worthless.

[3] Gaṅgā and Umā, being both daughters of the Himālaya, are sisters.

Within the mind of twice-born Rāmprasād there is this fear, that in this life I have not lived where dwell my Mother's family; and having had to live without my Mother's milk, my body has wasted. How long do you think the child will live if it is hand-fed?

A very obscure song. Our suggestion is that the 'aunt' is the religion of ceremonial and ritual, thought of as represented by Ganges, the co-wife of Kālī, Rāmprasād's 'Mother.' His experience of the exacting Hindu 'Law' has been St. Paul's of the Jewish 'Law.' But our colleague, Professor Ramsaran Ghosh, suggests that the 'aunt' may be *Māyā*, *Illusion.*

XLIX. NIGHT DRAWING NEARER

Going untimely, whither shall I go? I wander ever in a circle. Day has set, and my life, that sees this, is trembling. You who are the shelter of the shelterless, World's Mother, give me a place. I have heard Śrīnāth's saying, that you are the giver of the Four Goods.

Rāmprasād says: Remember, O remember this saying at her sacred Feet.

L. THE CORDS OF DEATH

Mind, thou has lost reality. By night and day thou sittest there, planning some means to get a well-filled purse.

My Mother Śyāmā is a hoard of gold for me; all else is mere deceit. Shame on thee, Mind! ill-starred art thou indeed, that for a paltry bargain thou couldst sell thy gold.

The cords of retribution have ensnared my mind, and who shall set it free?

Now in thy homeland, now abroad, a worthless vagabond art thou; an ill-fate was it that was written for thee.[1] Death lives within thy heart; its time speeds on as quickly as appear the young shoots of the *sāl*.[2]

Prasād says: Mind, what are thy thoughts? Thou art a horse that five[3] ride, and all the five do strive among themselves, each for his own. And thee they'll bring into confusion.

LI. DEATH AT HAND

Consider this, my Mind,[4] that thou hast none whom thou mayest call thine own. Vain are thy wanderings on the earth. Two days or three, then ends this earthly life; yet all men boast that they are masters here. Time's master, Death, will come and overthrow such masterships. Thy best-beloved, for whom thou art so terribly concerned, will she go with thee? Nay; rather, lest some ill befall the home, she will sprinkle with cowdung[5] the house where thou hast died.[6]

Rāmprasād says: When Death shall seize me by the hair, then, Mind, do thou cry *Kālī*, *Kālī*, and vain will be Death's purposes.

LII. AND AFTER DEATH THE JUDGMENT

O my Mind, what charge shall I bring against thee? Thou knowest how to say *śa* and *ba*,[7] but knowest not the names of Durgā and of Śiva. *Jilipīs*, *khājās*, *luchīs*, *maṇḍās*, *sarbhājās*,[8] all these hast thou eaten. But when I die, my Mind, then wilt thou learn the fun

[1] On thy forehead. [2] *Shorea robusta.* [3] The Five Senses.

[4] The reader will have observed that Rāmprasād often used *Mind* in the sense of *Soul*, as when Christ's 'rich fool' said to his *Soul*, 'Eat, drink, and be merry.'

[5] Cowdung is used in Hindu houses for purifying.

[6] The fear of ghosts is very widespread, and every effort is made to get a hedge between the living and the dead.

[7] These are shortened from terms of vulgar, almost obscene, abuse.

[8] Sweetmeats of various kinds.

of it![1] How can I keep house with the Five Senses, with their fivefold appetites?

O Mind, if thou dost steal and practise seduction, upon me must come the just punishment.

LIII. HE LONGS FOR DELIVERANCE

How long must I labour in vain?[2] Tārā, tell me, how long will you make me labour so? My purposes and actions are not one. Happiness comes never to me, my Mother. This body's Five Elements drag me five different ways. Mother, the Six Passions are their allies. Verily do I know what sorrow means. O Mother, I cannot choose that happy mind in which I should myself be happy. If thou feed me with *nim* and call it sugar, not thus will the bitterness go from my mouth.

Prasād, thou doctor,[3] why so distracted? Take refuge in Kālī.

LIV. PREPARATION FOR DEATH

Mind, why hast thou become a beggar? Thrice-wretched, knowing nought?

In search of the wealth that passes, thou art wandering from land to land. That which thou desirest, which thou lovest, seest thou not within thine home?

Mind, if thou but quit thyself like mind, thou shalt come to union. When worship comes easy and natural as thy breath, then death's poison will have no power upon thee.

The jewels and the wealth thy teachers have given, bind them fast to thee.

[1] This is sarcastic. Indulgence is not going to save him at the end.

[2] Like a brownie. See No. XXI.

[3] A reference to his caste, the doctor one (Vaidya).

This is the request of poor Rāmprasād, who hopes to touch the Feet that banish fear.

LV. HIS HELPLESSNESS

Where is any good for me? If there were any, would my mind wander in the paths of sin?

Ten-armed Goddess, Mother, look, my body is a burden in the world. I have not worshipped you with red hibiscus[1] blooms, with *bel* leaves, with Ganges water. Neither to Gayā nor to Kāśī have I been. But, when death comes to seize me, I will cry Kālī, and yet again, Kālī.

Twice-born Rāmprasād says: I am grass that floats on a stream. I cry out, Save me, Save me; who will bring me safe to shore?

LVI. KĀLĪ THE FENCE-MAKER

Mind, why art thou away from the Mother's Feet? O Mind, think on Śakti, thou wilt get freedom. Bind thyself with the rope of devotion. Mind, thou hast eyes but they show her not. Ah, what a burnt brow is thine![2] The Mother, tricking her votary, came in his daughter's shape and fenced his home.[3]

Our mothers' love is known at death. We die, and for two or three hours there is weeping enough, but at the end they sprinkle cowdung and finish. Brothers, friends, wife and children, these are but the roots of illusion. I die, and they send an earthen pot along with me, they throw eight cowries on my pyre.[4] They

[1] Offered to Kālī, because it is the colour of blood.

[2] What a luckless fool thou art!

[3] A legend current in the poet's lifetime. See p. 17.

[4] The coin of the very poor; sixteen are reckoned to the pice (one farthing). It is used only in tallies now, and is no longer a coin. Cowries are thrown along the road in funeral processions, and on the pyre; this is a nominal giving of alms.

take away my ornaments; all they take away. They put another cloth on my body, one that is square and full of holes.[1]

Mother, he that meditates on thee with steadfast mind, he wins thee. Ah, come out and see how Tārā, disguised as his daughter, is building a fence for Rāmprasād!

LVII. HE FACES DEATH

Death the thief is close behind thee. Awake, I tell thee then, my Mind, and slumber not. Take thy sword, the name of Kālī; thy shield is Tārā's name. Then, O Mind, shall Death be able to force thee to his will? The name of Kālī is sounding out its music. Mind of mine, call upon the name of Durgā, and turn darkness into day.

If Kālī does not save me, in this evil age when unnumbered sinners have been saved, is Rāmprasād a thief and worse than they?

LVIII. DEFIANCE OF DEATH

Herald of Death, get hence! I am the son of the Almighty Mother. Go, ask your Master how many like me he has seized. I can be the death of Death, if I remember the Almighty Mother's power.

Prasād says: Herald of Death, take heed what you say to me! Fellow, in Kālī's name I will bind you; and when I smite you, who will save?

[1] Literally, *cut right across*. This may be a reference to some funeral custom of Rāmprasād's time. We have failed to get an explanation.

LIX. THIS DAY WILL PASS

This day[1] will surely pass, Mother, this day will pass, and only rumour linger. Countless will be the reproaches against Tārā's name.[2] I came to the market of the world, and by its bathing-*ghāt* I sat to sell my wares. Mother, the Sun our Lord is seated on his platform,[3] the ferryman has come. The load of the many fills the boat, he leaves behind the wretched one. They seek a cowrie from this poor man; where shall he get it?

Prasād says: Stony-hearted Girl, look back. Give me a place, O Mother! Singing thy glory, I will plunge in, into the sea of the world.[4]

. . . . .

This song is recalled by Rabindranath Tagore in a well-known song in *Gītimālya* (see Fruit Gathering, 51); but that translation is only a brief précis of the Bengali, omitting the opening lines 'I know this day will pass.'

LX. HE HEEDS NOT MEN'S BLAME

Shout the name of Kālī, Kālī, folk say, and folk will say, 'He is mad.' Folk miscall you, will miscall you; let it go. Good and evil are two things;[5] do the thing that is good. Lift the sword of Kālī's name and with it cut down illusion and world's attraction.

Alas for the vain pull of this delusive world! It is bringing Rāmprasād to destruction.

[1] Some texts read, 'This brief day will pass,' with a play on *din*, day and *dīn*, brief, poor, obscured, 'This day will pass.'

[2] Because she has not saved her devotee.

[3] A conventional phrase for sunset, when the sun seems seated directly opposite the spectator; but the reader may recall the Musalman on his prayer-mat.

[4] The troubles of this life, over which we must pass to the next world.

[5] His protest against any philosophy which confuses moral distinctions.

LXI. HIS PLAY IS ENDED

My play is finished, Mother. My play is finished, thou Joyous One. It was to play that I came to the earth, I have taken its dust and played. O thou Daughter of the Mountains, now am I in fear of death, for death is close at hand. In childhood's days what games I had! Then I wasted in the joys of married life the breath that should have been given to prayer.

Rāmprasād says: Now that I am old and feeble, tell me, Mother, what I must do. O Mother of mine, thou that art strength[1] itself, give me devotion. Cast me into the waters of salvation.

This is another of Rāmprasād's poems that has haunted Rabindranath Tagore's imagination; his readers will remember many passages in his work which recall it.

LXII. AND HE IS FREE FROM FEAR OF RE-BIRTH

No more birth in this world shall I know, nevermore be in the womb of my mother.[2]

Call her Bhavānī, Bhairavī, Śyāmā, what you will—the Scriptures cannot contain her. Śiva alone has perceived her greatness. Countless are the sinners who have drunk of my Mother's name and found salvation. O Mother, show to me now Mount Kailāsa,[3] that heavenly dwelling-place.

LXIII. ALL ERROR IS ENDED

No more shall I wander and live amid error. I have rested all upon the Feet that banish fear, and with fear I shall not shake again. Weighted no more with the worldly passions that beset me, I shall not sink into the well of poison. Regarding joy and teen alike, I shall

[1] Śakti.

[2] The grace of Kālī has delivered him from the danger of re-birth in this world.

[3] Śiva's heaven.

no more carry fire in my mind. Drunk with desire of worldly wealth no longer, I shall not wander from door to door. I shall not clutch at the wind of hope, and lay bare my mind to others. Being now no more captive to the snares of sense, I shall not swing myself beneath love's Tree.[1]

Rāmprasād says: I have drunk milk, and even with my buttermilk I am not going to mix ink.

LXIV. CRYING TO KĀLĪ, HE WILL LEAVE LIFE

Will such a day ever come, when crying Tārā, Tārā, Tārā, I shall find my eyes streaming with tears? The lotus of my heart[2] will burst into blossom, all darkness will leave my mind. Then I shall roll on the earth, crying always on the name of Tārā. All difference and distinction I shall forsake;[3] my sorrows of mind will finish. The formless Goddess, who is more than many hundred Vedas, shall be my lot.

Śrīrāmprasād[4] proclaims: The Mother reigns in every vessel.[5] Look, blind eyes, upon the Mother, the Night-Dispeller who dwells in night!

LXV. THE END

Tārā, do you remember any more?

Mother, as I have lived happy, is there happiness hereafter? Had Śiva's words[6] been true, I should not

[1] Swinging has a religious significance, from its association with the Krishṇa legend.

[2] See notes to XI and XV.

[3] All religious perplexities will be gone, all worship will be simplified.

[4] *Śrī* is prefixed by a Bengali gentleman to his signature. It is often merely our *Mr.* or *Esquire.*

[5] In certain forms of Hindu worship each god is represented by an earthen pot filled with water. Rāmprasād holds that, whichever of the gods is worshipped, Kālī is the ultimate reality.

[6] The Tantric teaching of the efficacy of ceremonies and pilgrimage.

be beseeching you. After passing through delusion on delusion, I feel my right eyelid throbbing.[1]

Had there been any other place, I should not have besought you. But now, Mother, having given me hope, you have cut my bonds, you have lifted me to the tree's top.[2]

Rāmprasād says : My mind is firm, and my gift to the priest[3] well made. Mother, my Mother, my all is finished.[4] I have offered my gift.[5]

Traditionally, his last song. The text is even unusually doubtful and varying.

[1] When the right eyelid throbs, some ensuing gain is indicated ; the throbbing of the left eyelid indicates loss to come.

[2] To a position of isolation and great peril. The next step will be into emptiness. Kālī has taken away his ladder of belief in ceremonial, and she must now save him.

[3] The gift (in this case apparently, Rāmprasād's gift of his life-long devotion) when worship is ended. This gift is called *prasād*, so that Rāmprasād is punning to the last. 'Prasād has offered his *prasād*.' The *prasād* is sometimes kept by the priest, and sometimes distributed among the worshippers.

[4] Literally my claims are settled (adversely), dismissed. I have nothing ; but in that nothing I have all I need.

[5] 'I have offered my cock to Aesculapius.'

ASCRIBED TO RĀMPRASĀD SEN

LXVI. HE HAS WANDERED WITHOUT BEING WISE

Think, my mind! Today, or a century hence, you must die. Because your feet have wandered in the ways of the world, my Mind, you have not thought of Bhavānī.[1] Think ever of those Feet of Bhavānī, if you would pass hence to her world.

LXVII. CONQUEST OF SELF

Put fire to your passions, they will make fine ashes![2] Cleanse your mind with those ashes;[3] destroy the taints that foul it. Come to the lake of Kālī,[4] and get cleansing. The waters of that tank cleanse well. With sin for fuel, kindle a blaze, and place on it the brewing-vat of wisdom.

LXVIII. THE QUEEN OF THE BURNING-GROUND

Since thou lovest burning-grounds, I have made my mind a burning-ground, that the Dark Goddess, Dweller amid the dead, may dance there always. Nothing

[1] A line of puns and alliteration. Bhavānī is *The World's Mistress.* 'World-Explorer you have forgotten Her who is Herself the World.'

[2] The *Tantras* prescribe as places for meditation 'the solitary mountain-top, the lonely, empty house and riverside, and the cremation ground. The interior cremation ground is there where the passions are consumed in the fire of knowledge.' *The Serpent Power*, by Arthur Avalon, p. 217.

[3] Alkali that cleanses.

[4] A lake where she showed herself to worshippers. The story is told in Toru Dutt's *Ballads of Hindustan.*

remains in my mind, Mother, save flames of funeral ever burning. Against thy coming, I have scattered ashes everywhere.

Flinging beneath thy Feet him who is Time's Great Period[1] and Conqueror of Death,[2] come, Mother, dancing come, and, though my eyes be shut, I shall see thee.

LXIX. KĀLĪ THE REFUGE

Where'er thou art, O Bhava's[3] Queen, let me have sight of thee. Appear to me, thou wife of Śiva, disporting thyself on Hara's breast. Ever in my sorrow am I crying to thee, my Mother. Have mercy upon me, most merciful Mother. I know not how to worship; I am not worthy to worship thee. Thou saviour of sinners, let me behold thee. Thy wretched child, O Mother, crieth to thee. Thou who hast given me birth, forget not the day of my death.

[1] Mahākāla, *The Great Death*, *i.e.* Siva. (*Kāla*, as already explained, means both *death* and *time*.)

[2] Mṛituñjaya.

[3] 'He who is.' *Bhava* means *existence*, the *world*; and is also (like Hara) a name of Śiva.

KAMALĀKĀNTA BHAṬṬĀCHĀRYA

LXX. HE IS INDIFFERENT TO HIS WORLDLY FORTUNE

No matter what fortune thou grantest me, nothing is wanting if I forget thee not. Birth and labour and sorrow I take as sheer delight, if I but see Śyāmā's rain-clouds in my heart. A body smeared with ashes or decked with jewels and gold; a lodging beneath a tree or a seat on a royal throne—to Kamalākānta all are one, if thou, my Mother, make his heart thy shrine.

LXXI. HE IS ENTIRELY DEPENDENT ON KĀLĪ

I want nought else, O Śyāmā, save your two red feet.[1] And this boon I hear Tripurāri,[2] too, has taken. To see him thus possessed robs me of all my courage.

Relations, friends, my children, wife—all stay to share my happiness; but when ill-fortune comes, not one remains. I am become as those whose house is on the outskirts of the village.[3]

If by your own virtue you would save me, then look on me with kindly eyes. Else all this talk that by repetition of your name I may possess you is merest emptiness.

This is the word of Kamalākānta: I tell the Mother all my many woes. My rosary is in an old patched

[1] Her feet are red from treading the battlefield.

[2] Śiva, 'the enemy of Tripura,' a demon whom he killed.

[3] *I.e.* I am treated as an Outcaste.

bag,[1] and hangs there in the room where I have told my beads.[2]

LXXII. KĀLĪ'S POWER

O Kālī ever happy, delight of Mahākāla's mind, you dance for very joy and clap your hands in measure with your dance.

You are the primal element, immutable ; you are dark-hued as empty space, and wear the moon-sign[3] on your forehead.

From whence, before the world was framed, did you get your garland of heads ?

We act in this machine according to the *Tantra* rules, and you are the one mechanic.

As you have placed me, so I stay ; as you have taught me, so I speak.

The restless Kamalākānta reproaches you and says: This time, Destroyer of all, you have taken your sword and put an end to good and evil alike.[4]

LXXIII. THE POET'S GREAT HAPPINESS

My mind is a bee[5] sated with the blue lotus of Śyāmā's feet. The sweets of wealth are all despised, so too the flowers of passionate desire.

Black are her feet, black is the bee ; and black with black has mingled.

[1] Of *rudrāksha* berries, sacred to Śiva and Śakti. While telling his beads, a Hindu usually holds the rosary inside a small bag which covers his hand. When not in use, the rosary is kept in the bag.

[2] It is no use worshipping her, unless she attend to him ; so he abandons her worship.

[3] Kālī has a third eye in her forehead and under that the crescent moon.

[4] He is discontented and without peace of mind, and her activity seems to him merely destructive.

[5] The large black bumble-bee, a great favourite of Bengali poets.

See you, Five Elements,[1] drunkards beyond all others, you could not hold your ground when you looked on this happiness.

Kamalākānta's mind has at last been filled with hope; see how joy and sorrow have become one! The sea of happiness is overflowing.

LXXIV. EXTREME UNCTION

Listen, O Śyāmā, listen, O Mother, seated upon the dead, and let me tell you all my mind's desire.
At my last hour, O Mother, may this tongue cry, 'Kālī, Kālī.'
When they dip me in the water,[2] then, Mother, arise within my heart.
Then in my thoughts I will gather red hibiscus from the groves.
I will smear them with the sandal-paste of devotion, and present them a flowery offering at your feet.
Half of my body will be in Ganges stream, half will be on the land.
Some one will write upon my brow all the names of Kālī.
Some one will call aloud into my ear.
Some one will cry, 'Hari, Hari,' and clap his hands to keep time with his shouts.

By Kamalākānta, though it does not contain his name.

[1] Of which the body is made. These betray us into an intoxication of the senses; but the poet, engrossed in the worship of Kālī, is beyond the sphere of their power.

[2] When a high-caste Hindu is dying, he is, if possible, brought to the Ganges, and his feet are put in the water.

MAHĀRĀJA RĀMKṚISHṆA OF NĀṬŌR

LXXV. THE HOUR OF DEATH

When my mind is failing, then the name of Kālī whisper in my ears, as I lie on my bed of sand. This body is not mine, the passions sweep it along. O Forgetful One,[1] bring my rosary when I float in Ganges.

Rāmkṛishṇa, fearful, says to the Forgetful One: Thou art careless for my welfare, careless as to my fate.[2]

This song is quoted in Dr. Dinesh Sen's *History* (p. 721), but we found it first elsewhere.

One of the countless poems entreating aid at the time of death. The poet imagines that he has been placed in the Ganges to die; and he asks for his rosary of *rudrāksha* berries.

[1] Bhōlā (Śiva). But the poem will also admit of the explanation that the poet is reproaching his own forgetful mind, and not Siva.

[2] Literally, what is on my forehead. See note to XXIII.

RASIKCHANDRA RĀY

LXXVI. THE WORSHIPPER WILL CONQUER KĀLĪ BY HER OWN STRENGTH

Come, Mother, join battle with me as I worship.

Let us see, Mother, who will be conquered, the Mother or the son.

I mount the mighty chariot of virtue; worship and adoration, these two steeds are harnessed to it.

I have stretched the bow of knowledge; and here I sit, the arrow of devotion ready in my hand.

Today the battle shall decide the issue. What fear have I of death?

With beating of drums, I will seize the wealth of salvation.

In battle after battle you have overthrown the Daityas.[1] This time, O Goddess, come and fight with me.

Rasikchandra your votary says: It is in your strength, Mother, that I shall conquer you in battle.

[1] Titans. Often rendered *demons,* though they were not wicked except in the sense that they warred against the gods.

SĀIYĀD JĀFĀR

LXXVII. KĀLĪ CANNOT HELP HER WORSHIPPER

Why do you in such a plight call yourself merciful?
(This is the Mother, the merciful, and in such a plight!)
What wealth can you give me? You yourself have not even clothes.
Would a woman choose nakedness if she had aught with which to clothe herself?
Your husband is a beggar from his birth, your father is most cruel.
There is not in the family of either any to be a benefactor.
For Sāiyād Jāfār what wealth is there in your keeping? Hara's breast possesses your twin Feet.

The only interest of this song of somewhat ambiguous devotion is that its author is a Musalman. It is well known that Musalman thought has influenced Hinduism; but it is not so well-known that Hinduism, in Bengal, at any rate, has influenced Muhammadanism. Musalmans sing *Śākta* and *Vaishṇava* songs almost as freely as Hindus do; and *Vaishṇava* songs by Musalmans will be found in the companion volume to this one.

NĪLAKAṆṬHA MUKHOPĀDHYĀYA

LXXVIII. KĀLĪ IS THE UNIVERSAL OBJECT OF WORSHIP

Art thou Mother or Father to me, my Mother?

I have searched the Vedas and the Vedānta, the *Tantras* and the *Mantras*, yet nowhere have I found thy fulness.

As Rāma thou dost take the bow, as Śyāma[1] the flute: as Śyāmā the black, thou dost seize the sword.

Some offer at thy feet the *tulasī*,[2] some the *atasī*,[3] some come with handfuls of hibiscus, some bring the leaves of *bel*.

O Mother, Mother of the Universe, art thou male or female? Who can say? Who knows thy form?

In whatever form men think of thee, in that form do thou, Universal One, appear to them.

Nīlakaṇṭha's mind ever thinks of thee as chief amongst the deities.[4] Mother, if thou wouldst be Mother indeed, then why at my Mother's feet should my Father lie prostrate?[5]

[1] Kṛishṇa is called Śyāma, 'the dark one.' Śyāmā, a name of Durgā, is the feminine form of the word. It will be remembered that, when Durgā is first mentioned in Hindu literature, she is Kṛishṇa's sister (see Introduction, p. 11).

[2] Sacred basil, dedicated to Vishṇu. Almost every Hindu household and all *Vaishṇava* temples cultivate a plant. The poet is glorifying his goddess as the Supreme Principle, worshipped by others under the names of Rāma, Kṛishṇa and Śiva.

[3] The linseed plant; its flowers are offered to Durgā.

[4] Literally, *as chief of Creators*.

[5] Her station on Śiva's body is taken by the poet as symbolizing her lack of affection and compassion.

LXXIX. THE CALLOUS MOTHER

You are my Mother ; will you afflict me more ? I knew it not before, my Mother, that you are so hard-hearted : Had I known it, would I have called on you as Mother ?

You do not take your own child to your arms. Is this devotion to your child ? What other children are there anywhere who weep when they must call their Mother ? Stony-hearted Mother, you do not listen to your children's cries, you do not take away their pain. Born of the stone, a daughter of stone though you are, is it right for you to forget your children's anguish ?

Shame on you, Mother, shame on your evil ways, that in your mad delight you scatter about you the life-blood of your sons.[1] Who can understand what such a soul is like ?

Nīlakaṇṭha humbly says : Mother, as I behold your Feet, let not, at the last, death steal my spirit from its nest.[2]

LXXX. THE DEVOTEE VICTORIOUS

Come not here, Death, come not here. I have a dangerous snare ready for you. Kālī my Mother has given me courage, my fears have all departed. Now am I victorious everywhere, and Mahākālā[3] is defeated. The jewel of knowledge is bright within me. Kula-kuṇḍalinī[4] has wakened in my heart. No longer coiled up as a snake the Mother sleeps, but slowly, slowly

[1] A reference to her garland of human heads.

[2] Literally, 'snatch away my life-bird.'

[3] Usually a name of Śiva ; here used for the God of Death (with whom Śiva is sometimes identified).

[4] *The coiled one* (see note 2 on p. 50, also p. 12). When she wakens, she rises up through the spinal cord ; when she reaches the Brahmaraṇdhra (see note 2 on p. 45), the devotee's spirit is one with the Eternal, and, this identification being complete, passes from the body.

moves towards union with the Supreme. Glad at heart she goes to bring to nought the dangers.

O Death, close thine eyes and see that in my heart is Kālī's dreadful form.

Kaṇṭha says: So I say, come not here to fall into this snare.

RĀMCHANDRA DATTA

LXXXI. THE POET, IN PERIL OF DEATH, PRAYS TO THE MOTHER

O Mother, Hararamā,[1] when will you appear to me? Finished is this life's play, now let me have sight of you. Every day my body grows weaker, little by little the sight goes from my eyes. Now must you appear to me; if you delay, shall I have sight to know the face of Śyāmā?

I know you are present, Mother. Have you not cared for me? and clothed me? But what your form is like, this I do not know.

O Kālī, it is you who have put blinders on the eyes of your child.[2]

Anxious care has robbed my body of its beauty. Come, Mother, make yourself known to me.

If when my breath is spent and I am lying with my two eyes closed, if then you come, O wife of Śiva, tell me, what will your coming profit me? These eyes no longer will have power to see, and what my mind has thought my mind must keep.[3] No longer will these lips have power to call on you, my Mother.

My body is becoming as a stream whose muddy waters rush along in flood.

Will you not come to me, Mother, and wipe away the slime from me, your Rāma?

[1] *She who pleases Hara.*

[2] As with the oil-man's blindfolded ox (No. XXIX).

[3] Thought may still be there, but he will not have power to express it.

DWIJADĀSA

We cannot find out anything about the writers of the next seven poems, which are all popular in the villages of West Bengal.

LXXXII. THE WORSHIPPER LAMENTS HIS NEGLECT OF KĀLĪ

Never a day, never a day have you given me,[1] Tārā, Never a day when all day passes uttering Tārā, Tārā, Tārā, O Mother Durgā, the day goes its ill-omened way, spent in repaying my family's debts. Worldly desire goes not, your worship is not done, is not done. Not one day have I spent yet, crying only *Śaṅkarī, Śarvāṇī, Śivā, Śavasanā.*[2]

This is the prayer of Dwijadāsa:[3] O Mother Tārā, fill my eyes with bliss! Wife of the Eternally Happy One, keep me in eternal happiness! Floating in sorrow's stream, I waste away.

[1] Not a day of his life has been spent wholly in her service and praise.

[2] These are all feminine forms of names of Śiva. Śarvāṇī is from *śaru*, missile, arrow, and Śavasanā is 'she who sits on a corpse.'

[3] *The twice-born servant.*

ANONYMOUS

LXXXIII. A 'WALPURGIS' DANCE

Mother, Daughter of Giri,[1] why are you here at the burning-ground? Why in this guise?

Have you no shred of shame, that you can put your feet on Hara's breast? A naked, unclothed woman, you have set your feet on Hara.

Your tongue is hanging out, your curled hair falls disordered all about you.

You are Bhairavī[2] and Bhavānī, you are the cause of this world, and there you stand and chew the flesh your hand is holding!

The wine-cup[3] too you hold, and with the *yōginīs*[4] are dancing madly.

Such a poem as this shows what a furnace of aboriginal superstitions is blazing beneath the *Śākta* system.

LXXXIV. THE POET'S HEART A BURNING-GROUND

My heart I make a burning-ground; for burning-grounds you love. And Śyāmā who haunts the burning-grounds may dance there continually.

Mother, I have no other treasure in my heart, save the pyre that is burning there. Come, and you will see the ashes of the pyre scattered all about.

And him whose names are Mṛituñjaya and Mahākāla cast beneath your feet. Then come, O Mother, in your measured dance, and let me with closed eyes behold you.

[1] *The Mountain*. See the *Āgāmanī* songs which follow.
[2] Feminine of Bhairava (Śiva). See note to No. XXVI.
[3] Literally, *cup of Nectar*.
[4] Feminine of *Yōgī*, one who practises mental repression.

NAVAKIŚOR MŌDAK

LXXXV. DURGĀ IS FALSELY CALLED MERCIFUL

Can mercy be found in the heart of her who was born of the stone?

Were she not merciless, would she kick the breast of her lord?

Men call you merciful, but there is no trace of mercy in you, Mother.

You have cut off the heads of the children of others, and these you wear as a garland around your neck.

It matters not how much I call you 'Mother, Mother.' You hear me, but you will not listen.

Such is the kicking that all must endure, yet do men cry to you as Durgā.

ANONYMOUS

LXXXVI. AFFLICTIONS ARE HER MERCY

The sorrows, Tārā, thou hast brought and art ever bringing me, these I have learnt are only thy mercies, thou Mother who takest away sorrow.

It is for the good of the child that the mother chastises him; and so, my Mother, would I bow my head and submit to this burden of sorrow.

Mother, thou art the deliverer of the wretched and the guardian of those who take refuge in thee.

A grievous sinner I am, and so I have lost thee.

Tārā, I am as a bird thou hast tamed; I learn what thou dost teach me. Mother, thou hast taught me this word 'Tārā' and so I call thee, 'Tārā, Tārā.'

This song has been spread from Calcutta by the gramophone and is now sung throughout the villages of Bengal.

LXXXVII. THE SON HAS BUT ONE DESIRE

Śyāmā, my desire is satisfied.

Mother who art the joy of Hara's heart, and who dost bring to nought the hopes of men, thou hast made void what hope was left to me.

Though I place my soul an offering at thy feet, some calamity befalls. Though I think upon thy loveliness, unceasing death is mine.

Thou dost frustrate my desires, thou art the spoiler of my fortunes. Well do I know thy mercy, Mother of mine.

Great were my desires, and I spread them all out as a salesman does his wares. Thou didst see the display, I suppose, and didst bring confusion upon me.

Mother, the guards thou didst give me have looted my stall, they have not even left my capital.

My wealth, my honour, kith and kin, all have gone, and I have nothing now to call my own.

What further use is there for me? Wretched indeed am I.

I have sought my own ends, and now there is no limit to my grief.

Thou who dost take away sorrow, to me most wretched hast thou given sorrow. And I must all this unhappy lot endure.

Who will console the one who has no friend except his Mother, and whom that Mother makes to weep?

Make me to weep thou mayst, yet as I weep I shall cry 'Kālī, Kālī,' and with my tears I will wash thy feet. At thy feet I will roll in the dust. To lie there at thy feet and weep, that is my continual desire.

KĀṄGĀL

LXXXVIII. TRUE ADORATION

Śakti-Worship is not Merely Words

If it had been merely words, would not Bhārata,[1] a worshipper through all the ages, would not Bhārata through *śakti*-worship have lost its power? Just tinsel ornaments and crash of drums, not in these is *śakti*-worship to be found.

Offer the *bel*-leaves of a single heart, offer the Ganges water and lotus of devotion, and so perform your acts of adoration.

You may give your sun-dried rice, you may give your sweetmeats, but do not think that with these you can gratify the Mother.

Light the lamp of knowledge, offer the incense of an earnest soul; then only will that one who is divine fulfil all your desires.

Wild buffaloes and goats, these are the Mother's children; she does not want them as a sacrifice.

If you would offer sacrifice, then slay your selfishness, and lay your love of ease upon the altar.

Kāñgāl in anguish says: Where men make caste distinct from caste there can be no *śakti*-worship. Let all the castes be one and call to her as Mother, else will the Mother never grant us mercy.

Kāñgāl means *poor*, and is possibly an adopted name for the *baul* who wrote the song. Some of the most beautiful Bengali lyrics are the work of these *bauls*, many of them as anonymous as our English and Scots ballad-makers. A good collection of *baul*-songs is greatly needed.

[1] *I.e.* India.

ĀGĀMANĪ AND VIJAYĀ SONGS

THE DRAMA OF THE MOTHER'S RETURN HOME

RĀMPRASĀD SEN

LXXXIX. AN INCIDENT OF UMĀ'S CHILDHOOD

'Giribara,'[1] I can no longer try to quiet Umā. In angry pride she sobs and sobs and will not have the breast. She does not want the clotted milk; butter or cream she will not eat.

The night has almost gone, and in the sky the moon has risen. Umā cries: 'Bring it for me.'

No longer (I say) can I try to quiet Umā.

Her eyes are swollen with her sobbing, all tear-stained is her face. Can I, her Mother, bear to see her so?

'Come, Mother, come!' she says, and takes my hand; yet whither she would go I do not know.

Said I to her: 'You cannot grasp the moon'; and at the words she flung her ornament at me.

Giribara left his bed and sat him down, and tenderly took Gaurī[2] in his arms. Happy at heart and laughing as he spoke, 'See, little mother, here's a moon for you,' he said, and handed her a mirror. Great was her joy, as in the mirror she beheld her face, than countless moons more beautiful.

[1] Giribara, Sansk. *girivara*, chief of mountains, another name for the father of Umā.

[2] *Bright-complexioned* (Umā).

Rāmprasād says: Blessed indeed is he within whose house Earth's Mother dwells.

Umā's mother speaks.

XC. THE SAME CONTINUED

And as they talked, sweet sleep overcame Earth's Mother. Her father laid her on the bed.

At break of day Himagiri's queen[1] came to the shrine where Umā lay. Her being all intense with overflowing love, she waves the lights of happiness,[2] and calls her daughter back to consciousness.

The queen calls to her, calls, and calls again: 'Awake, little mother, awake. The sun is up, the night has passed. The sheldrake's mate[3] with her exulting song drives away her grief.

'Arise, arise, Gaurī, dear as life; Giri is standing near. No longer should you slumber.'

Poet,[4] rhapsodist and panegyrist with folded hands entreat you: 'Have done with sleep, have done with it, have done with it.

'You who are merciful, arise, and let me see your mercy,

'Go to Mandākinī's[5] waters; go, take you leaves of *bel*, and offer your worship unto Śiva.

'Listen, little mother, listen to your Mother's words.'

[1] Menakā.

[2] *Āratī*, a lamp of metal with several jets of light, which is waved before the image of a god morning and evening. Until recent times, this was commonly done to honoured persons in Hindu families. See Dubois, 148.

[3] When Rāma was lamenting the loss of Sītā, a pair of sheldrakes were joyously courting. He cursed them with eternal separation at night, but they are allowed to reunite each dawn.

[4] Court-poets awakened kings in Ancient India. This is an episode, while the poet in imagination adds his entreaties to those of Umā's mother.

[5] The river of Indra's paradise; the Ganges ere it descends to earth.

The smiles broke slowly over Gaurī's lovely face; she knew her Mother's voice.

The *kōkilas*[1] are singing, cold breezes are blowing.
The moon has no radiance now.
The water-lily sees her lord[2] robbed of his glory, and stands with saddened face, a shivering image.

The hapless Kavirañjana[3] says: O Durgā, who art merciful toward the wretched, save me, O save me, I pray. Look in mercy upon me, and deliver me from the waters of the dread ocean of life. Take me across to its further shore.[4]

This and LXXXIX are *from the Kālīkīrtan*; not an *Āgāmanī* song, strictly, but included here as giving a glimpse of Umā's early years in her mountain-home. The Western reader will be struck by the resemblance in spirit to the Homeric hymns; and in the first part in Rāmprasād's closing comment Persephone becomes Demeter. The translators cannot forbear to draw attention to the extreme beauty of the opening of the second part.

XCI. MENAKĀ HAS DISCOVERED UMĀ'S GREATNESS

My Umā is no common maid. Thy daughter, Giri, is not that, is not that. I am afraid to tell what I have seen in a dream. Oh, our Umā sat upon the heads of the Four-Faced[5] and Five-Faced[6] Ones. Queen of kings,

[1] The hawk-cuckoo, noisiest and (in the judgment of North Indian poets) sweetest-voiced of birds; clamorous in winter dawns.

[2] The sun is the lover of the lotus, the moon of the humbler water-lily.

[3] *He who pleases poets*; Rāmprasād's title from the Kṛishṇagar court.

[4] The conclusion, as so often, is a pious irrelevance.

[5] Brahmā.

[6] Śiva.

she speaks with laughing lips.[1] He, the dark-robed One, who rides on Garuḍa,[2] stands humbly in her presence, with palms together in supplication.

Prasād says: This is she whom sages cannot win by meditation. Blessed art thou, O Giri! What merit hast thou achieved to possess such a daughter!

Again, not an *Āgāmanī* song, but another glimpse of Umā's early years.

[1] As a child in Menakā's home.
[2] Vishṇu rides on Garuḍa, the great kite.

ANONYMOUS

XCII. A SONG TYPICAL OF THE ABUNDANT AND (AS IN THIS CASE) OFTEN ANONYMOUS ĀGĀMANĪ LITERATURE OF BENGAL VILLAGES

Menakā sends for Her Daughter.

Go, Giri, go bring my Gaurī; stricken with grief is she, my Umā. In my dreams I saw Nārada;[1] he told me that Umā was weeping most bitterly and calling 'Mother, Mother.'

Your son-in-law is a beggar and drugs himself with hemp. My Gaurī is an image, all of gold.[2]

I hear that he has sold all Umā's clothes and ornaments and with the money bought hemp for himself.

[1] The minstrel of Swarga (Indra's Heaven). Traditionally, he performs two functions: he sings eternally the name of Hari, and he foments quarrels everywhere.

[2] Gaurī means *bright-complexioned*, with the brightness of gold.

RĀMPRASĀD SEN

XCIII. THE JOY AT THE COMING OF UMĀ

Now has the happy night ended in dawn; behold thy daughter comes. Go, greet her entrance home again. Come, see her face beauteous as the moon! Your sorrows all will disappear. What stores of honey fall from the moon-beams[1] that are her smiles!

The welcome story heard, the queen hastes off, her hair dishevelled, her clothes all disarranged. Her streaming eyes are filled with tears of joy that well up from the floods of her emotion. She outruns Giribara, and, sobbing, falls upon her daughter's neck. Again she sets her on her lap, she gazes on that face most beautiful, and kisses her red lips. Says the mother: 'The mountains are your father, but your husband was a beggar from his birth. To think that I should give so fair a maid to Digambara!'[2]

Her girl friends come, their minds aflame with joy, and laughing take her hands and say: 'What have you done with that great love for us, that for a year you could forget us so? Come, lift your face and talk with us. Our life would soon have slipped away.'

Happy indeed at heart is Rāmprasād Dāsa[3] the poet. He swims in a great sea of joy. At the advent of the Mother all men rejoice. So lost are they in happiness that day and night are both alike to them.

[1] The moon is supposed to drop nectar. Cf. old English folklore; for example, *Macbeth* III, 5, 11, 23-25:

> 'Upon the corner of the moon
> There hangs a vaporous drop profound;
> I'll catch it ere it comes to ground.'

[2] 'One who wears no cloth' (because Śiva wears a tigerskin).

[3] Literally, *servant*.

RAJANIKĀNTA SEN

XCIV. A NEIGHBOUR GIVES TIDINGS OF UMĀ'S APPROACH

Arise, arise, O Giri's Queen, happy is the news I bring you, Mother; for, as I came, upon the road I met your Īśānī.[1]

Her grace illuminates the grove, she holds her two sons in her arms; a girl comes riding on a lion![2] More beautiful than countless moons are her twin feet. Her conch shell bracelets and her vermilion sign[3] alone adorn her radiant form. What need has she of ornament, who is herself as waves of light? Lest she suffer from the heat of the sun, a cloud overshadows her; the trees all bow their heads and, bending low their branches, fan her.

Along her path the flowers are bursting forth in ordered rows; the *kōkilas* are beside themselves as they sing their happy songs of the Mother's advent. From the trees the sweet fruits are falling at her feet. Saints and sages and the wise all are prostrate before her, and call to her 'Mother, Mother.'

O Queen, O Mother, I have hastened to bring you this glad news; now wipe away your tears and possess yourself in patience.

Kānta says: At the glad news Menakā is overcome with weeping. The holy water of such happiness purifies life from all its stains.

[1] Durgā. Feminine of *Īśā*—'Lord,' a name of Śiva.

[2] Girl and lion are almost the same word, the play on their sound assisting the antithesis.

[3] In the forehead, at the parting of the hair; the sign that a woman is married, and that her husband is alive. Conch shell bracelets also mark the married woman.

RĀMPRASĀD SEN

XCV. THE ARRIVAL OF UMĀ

'The City's all excitement, Queen, up and away, thy daughter comes to thee. Away, and welcome her and bring her home. Come, I say, come with me.'

'Jayā,[1] so happy is the news that you have brought, that you have made of me your purchased slave. All that I have you maidens may command. Come, come to me, and I will give my life to pay my debt to you.'

With quickening steps the Queen has gone, her hair all loose about her. Love bears her on, as water one who swims. All who approach she questions thus: 'How far off now is Gaurī, canst thou say?' On, on she goes, when in her path the chariot appears. She looks upon Umā's face and says to her: 'Thou art come, thou art come, little Mother. Hast thou, who art mother to me, forgotten me who am thy mother?[2] Surely that could not be, my love.'

Śaṅkarī steps from the chariot, bowing before her mother, and hastens in oft-repeated ways to bring her consolation.

Says Kavirañjana Dāsa in tender tones: Whoever else has known a day so fortunate?

[1] One of Umā's companions, who has come as herald of her mistress.

[2] This song is sung by the lady of the house playing a triple part; She is worshipping Durgā, is acting the part of Menakā, and is often remembering her own daughter, gone from her to a strange house, when but a child.

RAJANIKĀNTA SEN

XCVI. UMĀ'S MOTHER SPEAKS

Come, Guha[1] and Gaṇapati,[2] come to my arms. Still have these arms the strength to hold you both, a brother on each hip?

Long is the way that you have come, and you are spent. The radiance of your faces has been lost, as though behind a cloud two full moons lay hidden.

Then, too, among the mountains lay your path, a lion was your steed. Whenever was seen such suffering as this?

You know I send the chariot for you every year; I wonder what my mad son-in-law was thinking of to send it back. Alas, does any other let so fair a girl, such lovely boys, travel in such a way?

Let me kiss those soft cheeks of yours. Now let me feed you and your Mother, and give you clotted milk and butter to your hearts' content. I weep to think of all you must endure from want of food at Kailāsa.

Gaṇeśa, may you have wisdom in your speech! Kumāra,[3] of your great strength may the *asuras*, the foes, become afraid!

Kānta says: Śiva will live for ever, Mother, at your word.

Umā on her lion has brought her two sons.

[1] Guha (*protector*) is Kārttikeya, son of Umā and Śiva, and Commander-in-Chief of the celestial armies; the Hindu type of manly beauty.

[2] Gaṇeśa, the elephant-headed god of wisdom; in the popular legend (there are others), the son of Śiva by Umā.

[3] *Prince* (Kārttikeya).

VAIKUṆṬHA OF MĀLIĀRĀ[1]

XCVII. UMĀ REPROACHES HER MOTHER FOR THE YEAR'S NEGLECT

Pain is awake within my heart; what can I say, Mother? Am I no more as Umā in your thoughts? It must be so, for all this year that's past you have not sent to find out how I fared. Is it because of my unhappy lot that you have so neglected me? Day and night, Mother, I think about you; and, as I meditate, what anguish fills my mind! I would open wide my mind and show it you, were it a thing that you could see. See how constant grieving has robbed my body of its radiance. Is it because of my unhappy lot that you have no pity for me, your daughter? So it appears to me, my Mother.

Whom shall I blame? All know it was to a beggar's care that my Father and Mother gave me.

They who live in Kailāsa say to me, Mother: 'Have you no Father and no Mother, Umā?'

O I die with shame. What pretexts I have made! What stories I have told, to give the people some excuse![2] 'My Father Himāchala came to take me home.' Such are the lies with which I sing your praises!

I say to them: 'None of my own are with me here, with whom then could I leave my mad Digambara? Tell me with whom?'

Hear the word of Vaikuṇṭha, O Giri's Queen: 'What more can I say to bring consolation to the girl? Take your offended daughter to your arms: and as I gaze upon her beauty, my two eyes will be satisfied.'

[1] A village in the Bankura district.

[2] It is considered a shameful thing for a married woman never to be allowed to revisit her parents' home.

ANONYMOUS

XCVIII. UMĀ EXPLAINS HER INABILITY TO COME

You forget me, Mother, and all that I endured with my mad husband. Bhōlā is ever laughing and weeping and knows no one save me. He is always eating hemp, and I must stay near him. I cannot keep from worrying and wondering if he is safe or if any harm has come to him.

I have to lift his food up to his mouth, or he would forget to eat. There is nothing left of me, I am spent with worrying about this madman. I put him at his ease and came away, and then what floods of tears I shed, Mother. For I was fearful lest he go off alone, and none is so careless of himself as he.

DĀŚARATHĪ RĀY

XCIX. THE NEIGHBOURS COME TO CONGRATULATE MENAKĀ

Arise, arise, Mother, bind up thy hair. Here comes the daughter of the stone, here comes thy Īśānī.

Lovely as the moon thy daughter comes; she carries her two children in her arms; and, as she comes, she calls aloud, 'Where is my mother?' O Queen, the three worlds bless thy daughter, and in the three worlds there is none that can compare with her.

We thought she was Śiva's well-beloved; today we hear that she's thy daughter. Is it she, my Mother, who drives away the fear of the world? What mother has there been in all the earth as fortunate as thou, who didst conceive so fair a jewel in thy womb?

Mother, that star of thine is wife to Chandrachūḍa;[1] the brightness of the moon pales before her moon-like loveliness.

Such beauty I have never seen in any other; your Haramanomōhinī[2] takes away the darkness of my mind.

[1] The moon-crested one. See note to XXVI.

[2] She who has enchanted Hara (Śiva).

RĀMPRASĀD SEN

C. MENAKĀ WILL NOT SEND HER DAUGHTER BACK AGAIN

Giri, when my Umā comes to me, I will not send her back again. I will not heed the words of anyone, though men may say that what I do is wrong. If Mṛituñjaya appears and says that he would take my Umā, then mother and daughter will be quarrelling, careless of his being son-in-law to me.

Rāmprasād[1] the twice-born says: How shall I endure such grief? Śiva haunts the burning-ground and execution places, and has no thought for home.

CI. ŚIVA CLAIMS HIS BRIDE AGAIN

Giribara, Lord of my life, my body is quaking with fear. What dreadful story is this I have heard, that has turned my day into night? Mahākāla has spread by the door his tiger skin, and there he sits and calls, and calls again: 'Come out, O mother of Gaṇeśa.'

Hard as stone is thy body,[2] hard as stone is my soul; therefore all these days we have endured.[3]

Our daughter is another's wealth; we know this, yet we would not understand. Alas! Alas! is this how Vidhātā[4] doth mock at us?

Prasād's word is this: As, when the daylight comes, the *chakōrī*[5] despairs because his store of honey has disappeared, so, Himagiri's Queen, art thou made desolate.

A *Vijayā* song. Menakā is speaking to her husband.

[1] The poet, like a Greek Chorus, associates himself with the speaker in this drama. [2] He is Himālaya, remember.

[3] Literally, *have not burst.* [4] *The Creator.*

[5] The bird that feeds only on the nectar dropping from the moon.

RAJANIKĀNTA SEN

CII. THE MOTHER'S GRIEF TO LET HER DAUGHTER GO

Night, do thou stay; let not the dawn appear. Strike no more the wounded heart. Think once of what I suffer, listen once to what I say. Look in mercy upon me, so terribly stricken with grief.

O Time, rest that weary body of thine. Rest for a little while, 'tis not for long; rest for this night. Full well I know, thy wheel is ever turning; yet for today, my Lord, may it move slowly. O shining starry hosts, dim not this night your brightness. As the lamp's flame, shielded from the breeze, flickers not, so do you stay motionless.[1] When in the western sky you set, then comes the dawn; and when your light is dimmed, a thunderbolt will fall upon my head.

Thou rising sun of Daśamī, thou symbol of eternal cruelty, wilt thou now arise? Fate's executioner[2] art thou.

Kānta says: Rājmahishī,[3] that one whom saints and sages never knew, she has been three days within thy breast. Why, then, these tears?

Almost a *Vijayā* song. Umā's Mother is speaking, on the night of the ninth day after the new (*pūjā*) moon. Her prayer is Ovid's *Lente, lente currite, noctis equi.* The next day (*Daśamī*, the *tenth* day), Umā leaves her.

CIII. THE GRIEF WHEN UMĀ HAS GONE

Umā has left her unhappy mother. My sorrow cannot be measured with my tears. Alas! that none should understand my woe!

[1] Literally, *be like the pole-star.*
[2] Carrying out Fate's decrees. [3] *King's wife.*

Prostrate, I held her feet. How I wept! yet she would not take me with her. How can I go back again to a home bereft of Umā?

I know full well my heart cannot endure such suffering. I shall die of grief for Umā, or else become as one beside herself.

Since midnight on Navamī[1] Umā has been plunged in lamentation; today she put her arms about my neck and, weeping, took her leave of me.

With tear-stained, saddened face she says: 'Terribly stricken at heart am I, my Mother, to see your grief. My tears come flooding forth.

'Have you caught me in delusion's snare?[2] I cannot forget you. Yet there is no escape for me, so I must go. Think you my soul desires to go?

'Weep no more, Mother. I will come again. Then take this hope and tame your restless heart.' And, as she spoke, Umā wiped my eyes with the corner of her *śāṛī*.[3]

Even now before my eyes there floats the vision of that lovely face, radiant with tenderness, and faultless as the full moon.

These eyes of flesh will look on her again, yet such a thought is not enough to satisfy my heart. It is my Umā that I want. I want to see her, hear her, touch her.

Kānta, perplexed, wonders to himself: How will the year pass by? If you trust in Umā, Queen, shall you see autumn once again?

A *Vijayā* song.

[1] The *ninth* day.

[2] Umā, a goddess, is above the sphere of *māyā*. But her heart is so wrung at departure, that she wonders if she is being drawn into its net of illusive joys and sorrows.

[3] A Bengali lady's dress.

INDEX OF AUTHORS